PRINCIPLES OF
DATA PROCESSING

Third Edition

PRINCIPLES OF DATA PROCESSING

Steven L. Mandell
Bowling Green State University

West Publishing Company

St. Paul   New York   Los Angeles   San Francisco

COPYRIGHT © 1978, 1981, 1984 By WEST PUBLISHING CO.
50 West Kellogg Boulevard
P.O. Box 43526
St. Paul, Minnesota 55164

Library of Congress Cataloging in Publication Data

Mandell, Steven L.
  Principles of data processing.

  Bibliography: p.
  Includes index.
  1. Electronic data processing. I. Title.
QA76.M2748   1984   001.64   83-23499
ISBN 0-314-77923-X

ABOUT THIS BOOK'S
COVER PHOTOGRAPHS

The striking portraits of chips and wafers on the cover of this book were taken by photomicrographer Phillip Harrington. "The astonishing thing to me," says Harrington, "is that whenever I photograph computer elements close up, I discover entirely new vistas of beauty and colorful detail that I have never seen before."

Harrington, who was a staff photographer at *Look* magazine for 20 years, has in recent years specialized in macro- and microphotography. He does annual report work for such clients as General Electric, Schering Plough, C. R. Bard and Revlon; and undertakes special photographic projects for RCA and AT&T Technologies (formerly Western Electric). His work has also been featured on covers and multi-page spreads for such magazines as *Omni, Science Digest,* and *Medical Economics.* Harrington is a Fellow of the New York Microscopical Society.

The nine cover photomicrographs were taken with a variety of advanced techniques, among them fiber optics and an intricate polarizing prism system known as Nomarski reflected-light illumination. The photograph at center right shows, in actual size, a section of a chip-carrying wafer photographed with fiber optic illumination. At lower left is a single chip photographed using the Nomarski system, at 200 power. The chips and wafers were contributed by IBM, RCA, AT&T Technologies and the Bendix Corporation.

The microscope Mr. Harrington used is an Olympus research model equipped with incident light Nomarski illumination. Two cameras were used: (1) a computerized-automated 35mm Olympus system and (2) a Nikon Model F3 35mm reflex camera adapted for use with the Olympus microscope. The film used was Kodachrome 40 Type A, balanced for tungsten illumination.

PHOTO CREDITS

5, 6, 8, 9 courtesy of IBM. 10, 11 courtesy Sperry Univac. 15 courtesy of IBM. 16 (top) courtesy of Burroughs Corporation; (bottom) courtesy of Digital Corporation. 17 courtesy of AT&T Bell Laboratories. 25 (top) courtesy of Digital Equipment Corporation; (middle) courtesy of Tektronix, Inc.; (bottom) courtesy of Hewlett-Packard, Inc. 27 courtesy of Anderson Jacobson. 48 courtesy of Inforex, Inc. 49 courtesy of Honeywell, Inc. 53, 55 courtesy of BASF Systems Corporation. 59 courtesy of Anderson Jacobson, Inc. 60 courtesy of Interstate Electronics Corp. 62 Photo courtesy of DATA PRODUCTS CORP. 67 Armstrong World Industries, Inc. 68 courtesy of IBM. 69 courtesy of California Computer Products, Inc. 73 courtesy of Honeywell, Inc. 75 courtesy Itel Corporation, 77 courtesy of Xerox Corporation.

Preface

Computer systems have become an integral part of business, government, and society in a relatively short period of time. Academic institutions have recognized the importance of understanding computers and are requiring introductory courses in data processing for most students. The purpose of this book is to provide a brief but comprehensive overview of data processing principles.

Based on fifteen years of experience in introducing college students, business and government executives, and military officers to computer concepts, I have developed the approach incorporated in this book. The text material may or may not be used in combination with a laboratory experience gained through a programming language.

In a dynamic field such as computer systems, a book rapidly becomes dated. Therefore, this third edition, although coming just three years after the second edition, contains numerous technical advances. Significant improvements in the pictures and programming segments were given high priority. The section on systems was expanded to reflect the increasing effects of computers in society.

Many individuals contributed to the modified format contained in this edition. These changes were based on the extensive classroom experiences of teachers throughout the country. Several of these individuals warrant special mention for their efforts: Julius A. Archibald, Jr., State University of New York, Plattsburgh; George A. Bohlen, University of Dayton; John E. Nixon, University of Nevada, Las Vegas; Joe Z. Sollis, University of Mississippi; W. L. Staats, Hudson Valley Community College.

The text is divided into four major parts: (1) Information Processing, (2) Hardware Technology, (3) Software Technology, and (4) Computer Systems. The Information Processing section presents the basic concepts of data processing, including information flow and processing methodology. The Hardware Technology section concentrates on computer hardware from internal storage to selected input/output devices. The largest section in the book, the Software Technology section, is involved with computer software, especially program flowcharting and the programming process. Finally, the Computer Systems section provides a discussion of the application of computers in organizations and their potential impact. Section summaries, review questions, and a glossary are included to assist the reader.

The material in this book has been thoroughly tested by tens of thousands of students. I am indebted to all for their suggestions and comments. A special note of appreciation must go to Pat Cooke for her tireless involvement in the revision of this work. The background effort of Ann Clark continues to prove invaluable.

I welcome any comments or suggestions to continue improving *Principles of Data Processing*.

Steven L. Mandell

Contents

INFORMATION PROCESSING

PART ONE

1

HARDWARE TECHNOLOGY

PART TWO

35

SOFTWARE TECHNOLOGY

PART THREE

85

COMPUTER SYSTEMS

PART FOUR

125

PRINCIPLES OF
DATA PROCESSING

INFORMATION PROCESSING

Many individuals who think of the word **computer** envision an electronic marvel with mystical powers. In reality, the computer is a machine with capabilities that are quite limited, and its success can be directly attributed to the imagination of people. A computer possesses no independent intelligence. It cannot perform any tasks that a person has not envisioned or predetermined. Therefore, the computer's IQ is zero.

The number of different instructions that can be performed by a computer is also limited. These instructions apply fundamental logic and arithmetic procedures such as comparison, addition, subtraction, multiplication, and division to data items stored inside the computer. All of the procedures constitute the **instruction set** of the computer. They are designed into its electronic circuitry by the engineers who plan the machine. Computer power is then harnessed by the people who manipulate this relatively small instruction set; they use it to create computer programs. The major limitation to computer applications can be found in the humans who must determine the combinations of instructions the computer is to perform.

Computers derive most of their power from three features: speed, accuracy, and memory. Modern computers are capable of performing millions of calculations in a second. They are reaching the physical limitation of the speed of light. Error-free computation is for all practical purposes a reality, thanks to internal self-checking electronic features and the computer's tolerance for repetition. However, each computer user must realize that this accuracy relates only to the internal operations. What comes out of the computer **(output)** is correct only if what was initially put into the computer **(input)** was also correct. "Garbage in, garbage out" (GIGO) is a phrase used to describe the effects of incorrect input. Its meaning is fundamental to understanding computer "mistakes." The ability of a computer to store and recall information is almost unlimited. In addition, the physical size of data-storage devices is continually shrinking even though the storage capacity of these devices is increasing. The time required to retrieve stored information is also decreasing.

System Flow

All computer processing follows the same basic flow pattern. This pattern is shown in Figure 1–1. Output consists of the desired results in the appropriate form as determined by the users/customers of the computer system. In order for output to be generated, data must be collected and placed into a machine-readable form so that the data can be used as input. The computer-processing step then transforms the input into output through arithmetic and logic operations. Therefore, the development of the computer instructions necessary for the transformation is based on both input and output requirements. A set of instructions to the computer is called a **program.**

Figure 1–1 also depicts the relationship between data and information. **Data** is the facts, the raw material. **Information** results when that data has been organized and processed to be meaningful to some user.

This same basic flow is common to all data processing, whether a computer or a human does the processing step. However, when a computer is used, the processing is directly dependent on the capabilities

FIGURE 1-1 Data Flow

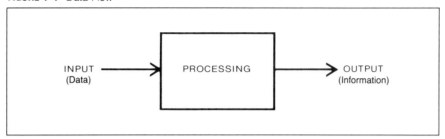

of its instruction set. This dependency forces the transformation of data into information to be both objective and mathematical in nature.

Computer Systems

A computer by itself is of little use to an organization. It can process data only after the data has been transformed into electrical energy. The computer stores and manipulates the coded data (which will be discussed in more detail in Part Two) by turning thousands of tiny switches on and off inside the machine. Obviously, this method of storing and processing data is quite alien to the numbers, letters, and other symbols used by humans for the same task. Therefore, a set of machines, called **input/output (I/O) devices,** must be present and linked to the computer so that communication between humans and machines can take place. Input devices are used to transform written language into electrical energy; output devices perform the reverse procedure.

The **central processing unit (CPU),** also known as the **mainframe,** is the heart of the computer system. It is composed of three units: (1) the **primary storage unit,** (2) the **arithmetic/logic unit (ALU),** and (3) the **control unit** (Figure 1-2). Each unit has its own separate function.

The control unit, as its name implies, maintains order and controls what is happening in the CPU. It does not process or store data. Rather,

FIGURE 1-2 Computer System Functions

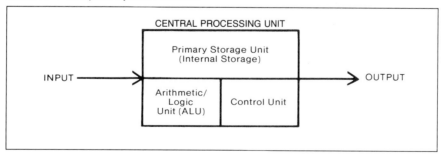

it directs the sequence of operations. The control unit interprets the instructions in storage and initiates commands to circuits to execute the instructions by producing the proper signals. Other functions of the control unit are to communicate with the input device in order to begin the transfer of instructions and data into storage and, similarly, to initiate the transfer of results from storage to the output device.

The arithmetic/logic unit (ALU) handles the execution of all arithmetic computations and logical operations. Since the bulk of internal processing involves calculations or comparisons, the capabilities of a computer often depend on the design and capabilities of the ALU. The arithmetic/logic unit does not store data; it merely peforms the necessary manipulations.

The primary storage unit **(internal memory)** holds all instructions and data necessary for processing. It also holds intermediate and final results during manipulation. Data is transferred from the input device to the primary storage unit, and held there until needed for processing. Data being processed and intermediate results from ALU calculations are also held in primary storage. After all computations and manipulations are completed, the final results remain in memory. The control unit directs them to be transferred to an output device.

A second set of devices, called **secondary storage,** or secondary memory devices, allows the computer to store large amounts of data and instructions in machine-readable code so that the computer can quickly access and use the information. Secondary storage is not located within the CPU itself.

A computer system is usually made up of a central computer linked to one or more peripheral devices—the input, output, and/or storage devices. A computer system, then, is a group of machines, each of which has a separate function. Since many types of computers and I/O and storage devices are available, an enormous number of unique computer systems is possible. However, several basic types of systems share common attributes. An organization should choose the system that best meets its processing needs.

HISTORICAL REVIEW

Humans have always used some method of keeping track of information. The progress toward the concepts of a computer and its supporting system extended over centuries, though many of the advances are recent. Often inventions in widely different fields found computer applications as the computer concept grew.

In the past, manual techniques of collecting and manipulating data were known as **data processing.** As technology increased and machines did the processing, the term **automatic data processing** was used. Now, technology has reached the point where an electronic computer can achieve the results formerly accomplished by humans and machines.

This is known as **electronic data processing (EDP).** Today the general term, *data processing*, nearly always refers to an EDP operation.

Background

The beginning of the climb to the computer concept using mechanical components began in 1642 with Pascal's adding machine. It used gears with teeth to store digits. When a gear rotated past the tooth representing the digit 9, the next gear to the left shifted one tooth, or digit (Figure 1–3). This concept was expanded by Gottfried von Leibnitz, who constructed a machine to add, subtract, multiply, divide, and calculate square roots. Mechanical technology continued to advance with the invention of more complex machines.

The weaving industry, of all unlikely places, was the site of the first machine to be controlled not by a human operator, but by a series of previously coded instructions. A loom operator had been required to constantly interact with the machine, adjusting the loom's settings before each operation. Joseph Jacquard developed a way to record each loom setting by using holes punched in cards. A particular set of holes in a card corresponded to one loom setting. Jacquard next designed a loom that could "read" the punched cards, or "instructions," and trans-

FIGURE 1–3 Pascal's Adding Machine

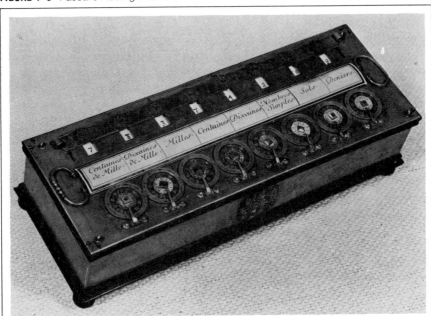

late them into appropriate loom settings. When a series of cards were linked together, an entire fabric could be woven without operator adjustments. This set of cards, or instructions, was the forerunner to the modern-day computer program.

In 1822, Charles Babbage developed the concept of a machine that could carry out complex computations and print results without human intervention. Using this idea, Babbage built a small working model of a machine called the **difference engine** (Figure 1–4). This machine was used to compute mathematical tables and gave results up to five sig-

FIGURE 1–4 Babbage's Difference Engine

nificant digits in length. When Babbage tried to build a larger model, he found that parts could not be produced to meet the necessary tolerances for accuracy.

Undaunted, Babbage thought of building a device that could perform any calculation—adding, subtracting, multiplying, or dividing—according to instructions coded on cards. This device, called the **analytical engine,** contained many features similar to those found in today's computers—in the early 1800s! An arithmetic unit called the "mill" performed the calculations, and the memory unit, the "store," kept intermediate and final results as well as the instructions for each stage of the calculations. Instructions and data were fed into the device by means of punched cards, and output was automatically printed. All of this, of course, was to be done mechanically, not electronically.

Although the analytical engine was originally conceived in 1833, Babbage died before it could be constructed. However, a model based on his drawings and notes was put together in 1871 by his son. To his tribute, it worked. Although Babbage was never able to see his inventions become reality, they nevertheless earned him the reputation of being the father of computers.

Working by Charles Babbage's side was Lady Ada Augusta Lovelace, daughter of the poet, Lord Byron. Ada Lovelace was considered a mathematical genius and her work with Babbage has earned her the title of the first programmer.

One of Lovelace's ideas was what we now refer to as the **loop pattern.** She had observed that the same sequence of instructions was often necessary to perform a single calculation. Thus, she discovered that if she used only a single set of cards and a conditional jump facility, the calculation could be performed with a fraction of the effort. Recently, a state-of-the-art programming language was named Ada in recognition of the many achievements Ada Lovelace brought to the development of computers.

The punched-card concept was put to good use in the late 1800s by Dr. Herman Hollerith, a statistician, to help the United States government process data gathered in the census. Hollerith developed the forerunner of what almost everyone recognizes today as the standard computer card. Each card had twelve rows and eighty columns and used a coding scheme that is still in use today. The use of the **Hollerith code** permitted specially designed machines to sort the census data according to the census' needs (Figure 1–5). Hollerith's invention reduced the time required to process the census from seven-and-a-half years to two-and-a-half years, despite a population increase of three million.

Hollerith's successful experience with the government led him to set up the Tabulating Machine Company which manufactured and marketed punched-card equipment for commercial use. His company later merged with others which, over time, became the International Business Machines Corporation.

FIGURE 1–5 First Census Tabulator

Early Developments to State of the Art

From the 1900s on, sorting out the various developments preceding the modern-day computer becomes more difficult, so quickly were they occurring. **Accounting machines** were developed in the late 1920s and early 1930s which supported full-scale record-keeping and accounting functions, but did little more than manipulate vast quantities of punched cards. The first real step toward the development of the modern-day computer was made with the **Mark I**, the first automatic calculator, designed around 1944 by a team headed by Howard Aiken of Harvard University (Figure 1–6). Instead of using mechanical gears like Pascal's or Leibnitz's calculators, it used electromagnetic relays and mechanical counters.

Electronic Processing During this time, researchers were studying the possibility of developing a calculator that used electricity rather than mechanical devices. An electronic calculator had the potential of supporting more complex arithmetical functions since it would not face the limitations of mechanically interacting wheels. It would rely on electricity rather than gears to operate much faster. The idea had some

FIGURE 1-6 The Mark I Computer

problems, however. For instance, numbers were easy to represent on mechanical calculators by the positions of wheels, but how could numbers be represented electronically? An electronic calculator has to rely on electrical currents to control and manipulate numbers, but only two electrical states are recognized easily: "on" and "off" (that is, either the presence or absence of current). A scheme had to be used to represent numbers using only these two states. The binary system, which uses groups of 1s and 0s to represent numbers, appropriately mirrored the "on" and "off" electrical states. Called "the language of the computer," or **machine language,** the binary system was used in these early experiments and is still used in modern computers. It is the only language that a computer can directly recognize and act upon.

The first true electronic calculator, called the **ENIAC,** short for the Electronic Numerical Integrator and Calculator, was developed only two years after the Mark I (Figure 1–7). A thirty-ton, fifteen-hundred-square-foot machine, it could perform a multiplication in three-thousandths of a second compared with about three seconds for the Mark I. Instructions to the ENIAC had to be given using a combination of switches, as no way existed for it to store instructions.

Not until John Von Neumann devised a method of encoding instructions electronically in the same fashion as numbers did storing instructions within the calculator itself become possible. This was an important development. The calculator could then execute instructions and perform calculations at its own speed, rather than rely on humans

FIGURE 1–7 The ENIAC

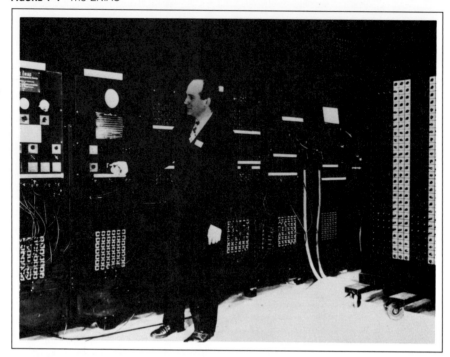

to direct each successive step. The ability to store instructions is one feature separating a computer from a calculator.

Von Neumann's principles spurred the development of the first **stored-program** computer. Two computers were developed around the same time using these principles. The **EDVAC** (Electronic Discrete Variable Automatic Computer) and **EDSAC** (Electronic Delay Storage Automatic Computer) performed arithmetic and logical operations without human intervention, depending solely on stored instructions. These computers marked the beginning of what is called the computer age. Further refinements after this time focused on speed, size, and cost. These developments are usually divided into four categories: first-generation, second-generation, third-generation, and fourth-generation computers.

First Generation: 1951–1958 **First-generation computers** were extremely large and had poor reliability. To control internal operations they used vacuum tubes, which were fairly large and generated considerable heat, much as light bulbs do.

Punched cards were used to enter numbers into the computer. These were cards with holes punched in them according to a coding scheme much like Hollerith's. A machine was used to interpret the punched holes on the cards and translate them into machine language for the computer. Machine language was stored as tiny magnetized spots on the outer surface of **magnetic drums** in much the same way that music is stored on audio tapes or cassettes. Read/write heads suspended just above the rotating surface of the drum either wrote on the drum by magnetizing small spots, or read from it by interpreting the already magnetized spots on the drum. Numbers were manipulated by the computer according to the instructions or program given to it. The results of these operations were punched on blank cards, which could then be read by humans.

The first computer to use all of these techniques was the **UNIVAC I** (UNIVersal Automatic Computer), developed by the same people responsible for the ENIAC (Figure 1–8). The UNIVAC I was dedicated to business data-processing applications. Thus, for the first time, business firms became exposed to the possibilities of computer data processing. Most first-generation computers were oriented toward scientific applications rather than business data processing. Scientific applications require computers that can manipulate numbers according to sophisticated formulas and keep track of the results to many decimal places. Business applications do not usually require such "number crunching," but involve rather simple calculations like addition and subtraction performed on large volumes of data.

The task of coding instructions for the computer using the 1s and 0s of computer language was extremely cumbersome, tedious, and time-consuming. During this period, **symbolic languages** were developed (Figure 1–9). These languages enabled instructions to be written using sym-

FIGURE 1–8 The UNIVAC I Computer

FIGURE 1–9 Machine Language versus Symbolic Language

MACHINE CODE TO ADD TWO FIELDS

11111010010000111000001000010100100000010101100

SYMBOLIC CODE TO ADD TWO FIELDS

AP   TOTAL,AMOUNT

---

bolic codes (called mnemonics, or memory aids) rather than strings of 0s and 1s. One word (or mnemonic) could represent a particular machine language instruction (a group of 1s and 0s).

The computer had to be given instructions on how to translate the mnemonics into recognizable machine language. This set of instructions was a program, too. What this program basically did was to tell the computer to look up each mnemonic given in a program and compare it against a list of all possible mnemonics and their machine-language equivalents. When the computer found a match, it took the machine-language code from the table. By doing this for all the mnemonics in a program, the computer was able to build a program in machine language that it could directly execute. The first such program for translating mnemonics into machine language was developed by Dr. Grace Hopper in 1952 at the University of Pennsylvania. After this break-through, most first-generation computers were programmed in symbolic language.

Second Generation: 1959–1964 In the late 1950s, tiny, solid-state **transistors** replaced vacuum tubes in computers. This greatly reduced heat generated during operation and made possible the development of computers significantly smaller and more reliable than their predecessors. These new computers were faster, had increased storage capacity, and required less power to operate. They were **second-generation computers.**

The magnetic drums of first-generation computers were replaced by **magnetic cores** as the primary internal storage medium. Cores are very small doughnut-shaped rings of magnetic material strung on thin wires. An electrical current passing through the wires on which a core is strung magnetizes the core to represent either an "on" or "off" state. In this way, groups of cores can store instructions and data. The advantage of magnetic cores is that instructions and data can be located and retrieved for processing in a few millionths of a second—faster than is possible with magnetic-drum storage.

This new internal storage of second-generation computers was often supplemented by another form of storage that used magnetic tapes.

Magnetic tapes are very much like recording tapes used for music, only wider. Magnetic tapes provided faster loading of data into the computer than was possible with punched cards. The results of computer operations could also be stored faster by placing results on tape rather than on cards.

Along with refinements in hardware technology, second-generation computers also were characterized by further refinements in programming languages. Second-generation computers often used high-level languages to instruct the computer how to perform processing tasks. **Higher-level languages** resemble English a lot more than symbolic languages do, and hence are easier to use. The first high-level language to achieve widespread acceptance was called **FORTRAN** *(FORmula TRANslator)*, developed in the mid–1950s by IBM. Because FORTRAN lacked many features desirable for business data processing, another language called **COBOL** *(COmmon Business-Oriented Language)* was developed in the early 1960s. This language was geared toward processing large amounts of business transactions easily. See Figure 1–10 for a comparison between a high-level and a symbolic language.

Third Generation: 1965–1971 Continued technological advances in electronics and solid-state devices brought further reductions in computer size, even greater reliability and speed, and lower costs. **Integrated circuits** replaced the transistors of second-generation equipment in machines referred to as **third-generation computers** (Figure 1–11). Through techniques like etching and printing, hundreds of electronic components could be included on silicon circuit chips less than one-eighth-inch square.

The transition from the second to the third generation occurred when IBM introduced the System/360 computers. This family, or series, consisted of six different computers, each offering a different main-storage capacity. The series was designed to provide all types of processing; its computers were capable of supporting forty different input/output and auxiliary storage devices. Within a short time after the introduction of the System/360, other manufacturers announced their versions of third-generation computers. RCA, Honeywell, Univac, Burroughs, and others began competing with IBM; and before long, more than 25,000 third-generation computer systems were installed throughout the United States (Figure 1–12).

The advances in solid-state technology that led to third-generation computers also led to the emergence of minicomputers (Figure 1–13). **Minicomputers** offer many of the same features of full-scale computer systems (such as the IBM System/360) but on a smaller scale. They are physically smaller with less main-storage capacity. They nevertheless provide a powerful computer system and a cost-efficient alternative for small businesses. A small computer manufacturer called Digital Equipment Corporation (DEC) introduced the first commercially accepted minicomputer in 1965 and has since grown into the largest manufacturer of minicomputers in the United States.

FIGURE 1–10 Comparison of High-Level and Symbolic Languages

```
SYMBOLIC LANGUAGE   Excerpt from payroll program in Assembly Language

OVERTIME    AP       OVRTME,FORTY          ⎫
            MP       OVRTME,WKRATE         ⎪
            AP       GROSS,WKRATE          ⎪
            SP       WKHRS,FORTY           ⎬  Computer
            MP       WKHRS,ONEHLF          ⎪  Overtime
            MP       GROSS,WKHRS           ⎪  Pay
            MVN      GROSS+5(1),GROSS+6    ⎪
            ZAP      GROSS(7),GROSS(6)     ⎪
            AP       GROSS,OVRTME          ⎭
TAXRATE     CP       GROSS,=P'25000'       ⎫
            BH       UPPERRTE              ⎪  Determine
            ZAP      RATE,LOW              ⎬  Tax Rate
            B        TAXES                 ⎪
UPPERRTE    ZAP      RATE,HIGH             ⎭
TAXES       ZAP      TOTAXES,GROSS         ⎫
            MP       TOTAXES,RATE          ⎪
            AP       TOTAXES,=P'50'        ⎬  Compute
            MVN      TOTAXES+5(1),TOTAXES+6⎪  Taxes
            ZAP      TOTAXES(7),TOTAXES(6) ⎭
            SP       GROSS,TOTAXES         ⎫  Calculate Net Pay
            MVC      PRPAY,MASK            ⎬  and Edit Print Line
            ED       PRPAY,GROSS           ⎭
            MVC      PRNAME,NAME           ⎫  Print Output Line
            XPRNT    LINE,32               ⎭
```

HIGH-LEVEL LANGUAGE   Excerpt from payroll program in COBOL Language

```
OVERTIME-ROUTINE.
    MULTIPLY WAGE-PER-HOUR BY 40 GIVING REGULAR-PAY.
    SUBTRACT 40 FROM HOURS-WORKED GIVING OVERTIME-HOURS.
    MULTIPLY WAGE-PER-HOUR BY 1.5 GIVING OVERTIME-RATE.
    MULTIPLY OVERTIME-HOURS BY OVERTIME-RATE GIVING
        OVERTIME-PAY.
    ADD REGULAR-PAY, OVERTIME-PAY GIVING GROSS-PAY.
TAX-COMPUTATION.
    IF GROSS-PAY IS GREATER THAN 250 THEN MULTIPLY GROSS-PAY
        BY 0.20 GIVING TAX ELSE MULTIPLY GROSS-PAY BY 0.14
        GIVING TAX.
    SUBTRACT TAX FROM GROSS-PAY GIVING NET-PAY.
    MOVE EMPLOYEE-NAME TO NAME.
    MOVE NET-PAY TO AMOUNT.
    WRITE PRINT-LINE.
    GO TO WORK-LOOP.
```

Another third-generation innovation involved **remote terminals**—terminals placed at various geographical locations and used to communicate directly (to be **online**) with a central computer. Using such terminals, many people can access the central computer at the same time and receive almost instantaneous results.

FIGURE 1–11 First-, Second-, and Third-Generation Components

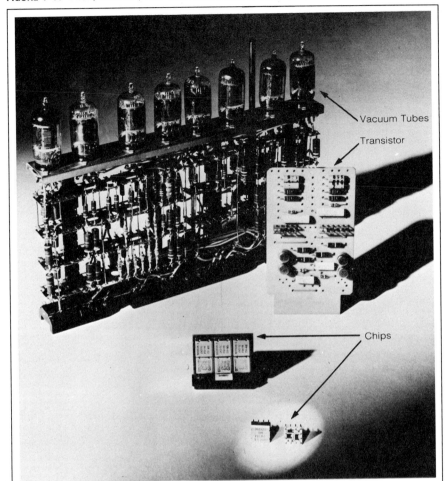

Fourth Generation: 1972–? After the introduction of third-generation computers, further technological developments have not been so clearly defined. Some academicians argue that fourth-generation computers are represented by IBM's System/370 computers. In these computers, electronic components were further miniaturized through **large-scale integrated (LSI) circuits.** This process puts thousands of transistors on a single silicon chip. These new LSI chips have replaced magnetic cores as the primary storage medium and provide faster processing speeds.

Another academic group supports the idea that microtechnology itself is the fourth generation. LSI technology made possible the development of **microprocessors,** which appear in devices people use every

FIGURE 1–12 A Third-Generation Computer System

FIGURE 1–13 A DEC Minicomputer That Uses
Third-Generation Miniaturization Techniques

day (Figure 1–14). Many microwave ovens, sewing machines, thermostats, and even late-model automobiles use microprocessors to govern their operations. By using the microprocessor in combination with other LSI chips, scientists have developed an extremely small computer called a **microcomputer.** Microcomputers are now being used in the home for such things as maintaining Christmas card lists, keeping track of recipes, and amusing people with games.

As time progresses, LSI is being replaced by VLSI (very-large-scale integration), which is now being perfected by scientists and engineers. This means that computers will become smaller still. Table 1–1 summarizes the advancements of computers according to generation.

PROCESSING CONCEPTS

Most business processing consists of updating data files and using these files to generate reports. In general, this processing can be accomplished in two ways. The data files can be updated on a regularly scheduled basis using whatever new data has been collected since the last update. This method is known as **batch processing.** Alternatively, the files can be updated immediately whenever new data is available, through a

FIGURE 1–14 Bell Lab's Newest Chip

TABLE 1–1 Computer Advancements

PERIOD	COMPUTER-SYSTEM CHARACTERISTICS
First Generation 1951 – 1958	Use of vacuum tubes in electronic circuits Magnetic drum as primary internal-storage medium Limited main-storage capacity Slow input/output; punched-card-oriented Low-level symbolic-language programming Heat and maintenance problems Applications: payroll processing and record keeping Examples: IBM 650 UNIVAC I
Second Generation 1959 – 1964	Use of transistors for internal operations Magnetic core as primary internal-storage medium Increased main-storage capacity Faster input/output; tape orientation High-level programming languages (COBOL, FORTRAN) Great reduction in size and heat generation Increased speed and reliability Batch-oriented applications: billing, payroll processing, updating inventory files Examples: IBM 1401 Honeywell 200 CDC 1604
Third Generation 1965 – 1971	Use of integrated circuits Magnetic core and solid-state main storage More flexibility with input/output; disk-oriented Smaller size and better performance and reliability Extensive use of high-level programming languages Emergence of minicomputers Remote processing and time-sharing through communication Availability of operating-system programs (software) to control I/O and do many tasks previously handled by human operators Applications: airline-reservation system, market forecasting, credit-card billing Examples: IBM System/360 NCR 395 Burroughs B5500
Fourth Generation 1972 – ?	Use of large-scale integrated circuits Increased storage capacity and speed Modular design and compatibility between equipment (hardware) provided by different manufacturers (customer no longer tied to one vendor) Availability of sophisticated programs for special applications Greater versatility of input/output devices Increased use of minicomputers Introduction of microprocessors and microcomputers Applications: mathematical modeling and simulation, electronic funds transfer, computer-aided instruction, and home computers Examples: IBM 3033 Burroughs B7700 HP 3000 (minicomputer)

method called **online processing**. Each type of processing has its own advantages. The type of processing required will greatly influence the type of computer system selected by an organization.

Data Hierarchy

Before data-processing methods can be discussed, the concept of data organization should be examined. A hierarchy of data exists in any organization, starting with small units of data that are grouped into successively larger categories. The basic unit of data in computer operations is the **bit**, one binary digit, which is either a 0 or a 1. Bits go together to form **bytes** to represent alphabetic or numeric characters and symbols. Groups of characters then are assigned to particular **fields.** If an organization were, for instance, collecting data about its employees, such fields as name, address, and social-security number would probably be used. A field is a unit of data that is not very meaningful when broken down any further. A collection of related fields is called a **record**—the next highest unit of data. An employee record would consist of all the fields pertaining to a single employee. A group of related records defines a data **file.** All of a firm's employee records would make up the firm's employee file. Figure 1–15 illustrates how fields and records are built into files.

Organizations possess many data files. Examples are employee, customer, and inventory files. When these files are structured so that the

FIGURE 1–15 Employee Data—ABC Company

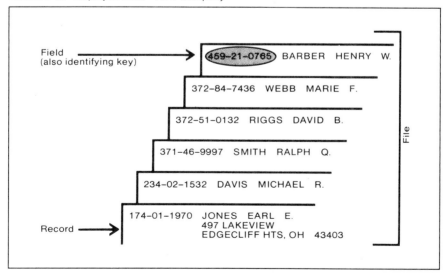

computer can access several files nearly simultaneously, the files are said to be integrated. For instance, the computer may be instructed to access both inventory and customer files for the purpose of customer billing. When organized in such a manner, the firm's integrated files make up a **data base** (Figure 1–16).

Sequential Processing

Batch processing is used by an organization when a periodic updating of files is acceptable. New data used in the updating process is batched or collected between updates. This method of updating is usually linked with **sequential processing.** Prior to the updating run, the collection of new data is sorted so that the sequence of the data matches the order of data already stored in the data file. The file then can be updated according to the sequence of data in the original file.

Illustration Figure 1–17 illustrates the chain of events taking place in batch/sequential processing. The collection of new data is called the **transaction file.** Prior to processing, the transaction file is sorted to match the sequence of the original file, called the **master file.** Data in the transaction file must be put into machine-readable form. In this case, the data is stored on magnetic tape. The transaction file and the master file are then processed together. Records in the two files are compared to determine whether a match has taken place. A special field,

FIGURE 1–16 Organization of Data

	Example
Data Base	All organization files
File	All employee records
Record	All fields about one employee
Field	Employee name
Character	Symbols used in the name, usually a byte
Bit	One binary digit; several are necessary to code each character

the **key field,** is checked, to ensure that the proper record has been found. The key field positively identifies a record since the data found in this field should be unique to each record. In an employee file, for example, the social-security number is often used as the key field because, although two employees may have the same name, no two employees will have the same social-security number. When a record on the master file that matches a record on the transaction file is found, the file is updated

FIGURE 1–17 Batch Processing

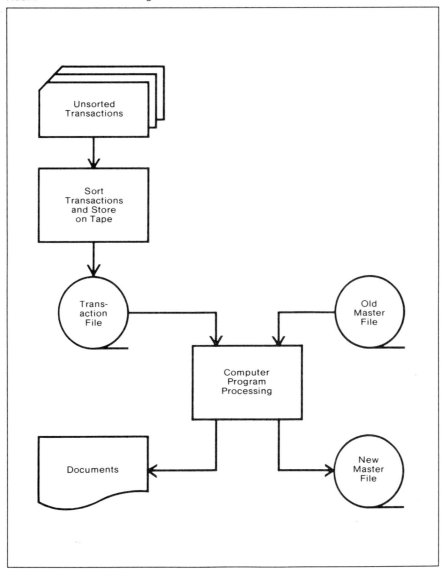

with the new data and placed on a new master file. Output from processing includes the new, updated master file and any reports that may be desired. The old master file is not changed by the processing.

Batch processing is best suited to those applications in which regularly scheduled reports are desired. An application such as the processing of payroll is ideally suited to batch processing since, typically, a payroll is prepared on regularly scheduled dates. The transaction file might consist of time cards that have been collected since the last payroll.

Pros and Cons The primary advantage of batch processing is that it is economical and efficient in terms of both machine and personnel time as long as relatively large amounts of data are being processed each time. Another important advantage of batch processing is that if the current master file is somehow destroyed (say, by accidental erasure), it can be reconstructed by processing the old master file and the transaction file. Thus, batch processing is somewhat secure, since a natural backup system for regenerating lost data files exists. The primary disadvantage of batch processing is that transaction records become dated as they are being collected. Thus the current master file is actually never quite up-to-date. Whether or not this is a serious problem depends on the application.

Originally, the storage media used with batch processing were punched cards or magnetic tapes. The nature of these media dictated the need for sequential processing because when files are stored on tape or cards, processing must start at the beginning of the file and continue until the end is reached. Even if only one record is being processed, the whole master file must be read by the computer. Consequently, the procedure of batching records was instituted in order to make the processing run worthwhile. Thus, batch processing became associated with sequential storage media. Today, computer systems based on **magnetic-disk** storage are becoming more popular than tape- or card-based systems. The advantage of disks, which resemble phonograph records without the grooves, is that only those records actually being updated need to be processed or read by the computer. Although disks eliminate the necessity of sequential processing, batch processing is being used with disks and other devices for reasons of economy and security.

Direct-Access Processing

In contrast to sequential processing, **direct-access processing** does not require grouping or sorting of transaction records prior to processing. Data can be submitted to the computer in the order in which events occur. The advent of the **direct-access storage device (DASD),** such as magnetic disks mentioned previously, has made this type of processing possible. A particular record on a master file can be accessed directly and updated without the computer having to read all the preceding records on the file. The result is that the information in the master file can be kept as current as the most recent transaction.

Illustration   Figure 1–18 illustrates direct-access processing **(random-access processing).** The data from a transaction is entered into the computer when the transaction occurs. The computer is programmed to find and update the appropriate record on the DASD. As is the case with sequential processing, a unique key is needed to identify the correct record. Unlike sequential processing, though, only the record to be updated is accessed; all others are ignored.

One use of a direct-access system is for airline reservations. Coordination of sales efforts is required so that a passenger in Cleveland and one in Detroit do not purchase the same seat on the same flight to New York. With the direct-access systems a ticket agent can submit a flight number and the quantity of seats required on the flight, and obtain the necessary information quickly. This can be achieved because the information about all flights from the start of the file to the desired flight record does need to be read; only the flight in question is checked and changed. The computer system has an up-to-date report on all flights at all times.

Pros and Cons   Direct-access processing is much faster than batch/sequential processing when only a small number of records must be accessed, since preliminary sorting is not required and the complete master file does not have to be read during the processing run. Precautions needed to avoid potential security problems are different with direct-access updating because a new master file is not written each time. The master is updated but never totally rewritten. To provide backup, an organization may, for example, make a tape copy of the master file once a week and keep the current weekly transactions so that the file can be reconstructed if necessary.

FIGURE 1–18   Direct-Access Processing

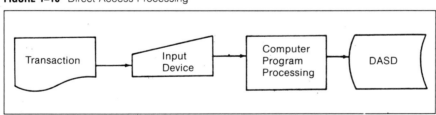

SOPHISTICATIONS IN SYSTEM DESIGN
Online Processing

Online processing refers to data processing using equipment—input, output, and storage devices—in direct communication with the computer to permit immediate data entry and retrieval. Whenever a computer can return information fast enough to affect a decision at hand, as in the case of handling airline reservations, the system is said to be operating in **real time.**

In an online system, **terminals** generally are used to enter and retrieve data from the computer (Figure 1–19). A terminal is an input/output device that may be located near the computer or at a location remote from it. Remote terminals are linked to the computer through telecommunications sytems. Many types of terminals are available to meet the needs of various applications; thus, the types of terminals used vary with the needs of the organization.

Teleprocessing

Terminals may be some distance away from the main computer. The combined use of communication facilities, such as telephone systems and data-processing equipment, is known as **teleprocessing.** Teleprocessing allows organizations to place data-entry devices where data originates and to locate output devices where the output is needed. The computers used in handling airline reservations are part of a telecommunications system. Terminals located at reservations counters throughout the world are all linked to a central bank of computers.

Terminals can be connected to the computer in a variety of ways. If the terminal is relatively close, a direct wire connection can be made. More commonly, the terminals are part of a large communications network. When telephone lines are used to transmit data, organizations can either lease private lines or use the conventional and less expensive public dial-up service.

Message Transmission

Form of Transmission Data can be transmitted over communication channels in one of two forms: analog or digital. Transmission of data in continuous wave form is referred to as **analog transmission.** This is the type of transmission used on normal telephone lines. An analog transmission can be likened to the waves created by a stick in a pan of still water. By sending "waves" down a wire electronically, one causes messages to be sent and received. In the past, analog transmission was the major means of relaying data over long distances. This was largely because of the type of communication lines provided by American Telephone and Telegraph (AT&T). **Digital transmission** involves transmit-

FIGURE 1–19 Computer Terminals

ting data as distinct "on" and "off" states; it represents data in the same form the computer does (Figure 1–20).

Analog transmission requires that the sender convert the data from the digital (on/off) form in which the data is stored to analog (wave) form before transmitting. This conversion process is called **modulation.** The opposite conversion—from wave form to digital—is required at the receiving end before the data is entered into the computer. This con-, version is called **demodulation.** Both modulation and demodulation are accomplished by devices called **modems** (Figure 1–21). The term *modem* is derived from the terms *mod*ulation and *dem*odulation.

Digital transmission requires no conversion of data, since the computer stores data in pulse form. This reduces the time required to send messages. Digital transmission also results in fewer transmission errors. These two facts mean that users can exchange large amounts of data faster and more reliably using digital, rather than analog, transmission.

Satellite Communication Systems Today many computer systems rely on the use of satellite communication channels to extend their ranges to other continents. Satellite-based networks are very expensive, primarily because they need earth stations (small dishlike antennae) to send and receive messages from the satellites. In the past, satellites were used mainly for voice and television tⴢransmission. However, satellite communication is becoming increasingly attractive for business applications. Satellites are used by dispersed companies to save time and money in the transfer of voice and data, since communication can be extended across the country or across the world (Figure 1–22).

In the development of satellites over the last two decades, several problems have emerged that do not exist with terrestrial networks. Although satellite communication is a cost-effective method for large companies, it is a very capital- and equipment-intensive industry, and satellites must compete with AT&T's existing land-based network. It is generally agreed that satellites are not a substitute for gound networks.

FIGURE 1–20 Analog and Digital Transmission

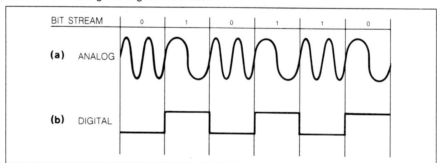

FIGURE 1–21 Modem

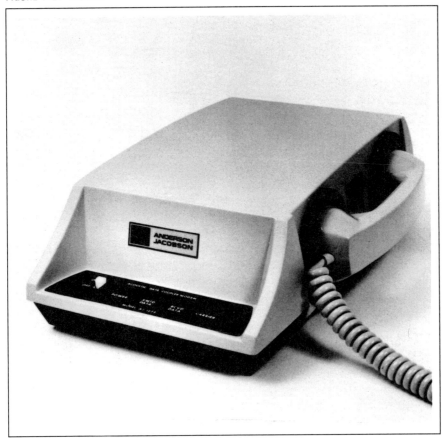

Measures must be taken to guard against such things as time delays (caused by the large distances the signals must cross), **downtime** (the time the system is not working because of equipment problems), security problems, natural disasters, and even war. And since satellites are often connected to land-based networks, precautions must be taken to avoid possible incompatibility.

Timesharing

Frequently in online systems, many users are working with the same central computer at the same time. Since each user is getting nearly instantaneous responses to his or her instructions, it seems as if each user has complete control over the computer. Actually, each user is sharing the same computer. **Timesharing** is the process whereby the computer's time is divided among many users at the same time. Since

FIGURE 1–22 Satellite Communications

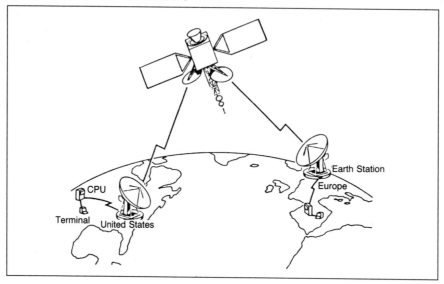

the response time of the computer is many times faster than the response of a human, it appears as though the computer is performing many tasks simultaneously. A computer can do only one thing at a time, but it works very quickly. Both remote and local users can timeshare on the same machine.

Growth in the timesharing industry is primarily a result of the advances in data-communication equipment. Timesharing customers usually purchase input/output devices and use them to access the facilities of the timesharing company. Storage space on magnetic tapes and disks can be rented; the customer pays for CPU resources at a monthly rate. Some timesharing companies have networks of computers spread throughout the nation. They have the ability to distribute the costs of such a system over many users, thus reducing overall costs.

A disadvantage of using timesharing is that it becomes very expensive as data-processing needs increase. The more computer time required, the greater the monthly costs. However, timesharing may be an economical alternative for companies that are first-time EDP users.

SUMMARY

● A computer is a general-purpose, information-processing machine that derives its power from speed, accuracy, and memory. The basic flow pattern of all computer processing is input, processing, and output.

● Data is unprocessed, unorganized facts. Once processed, this raw material becomes information of use to a decision maker.

● A computer system is generally composed of a central computer linked to various peripheral devices that perform input, output, and storage functions.

● The central processing unit (CPU) of a computer has three parts: the control unit, primary storage, and the arithmetic/logic unit.

● Storage within the CPU is called primary or internal memory. Additional memory space can be provided by secondary storage devices.

● For a long time humans have been preoccupied with calculating the answers to problems and keeping track of the results. Developments preceding the computer that illustrate this trend include Pascal's and Leibnitz's calculating machines and Babbage's difference engine.

● The weaving industry was the site of the first "programmable" machine, using punched cards to instruct the loom. Hollerith later applied this concept in processing census data, developing machines that could read data punched onto cards. Accounting machines applied the same techniques for processing business data.

● The Mark I was the first automatic calculator, and the ENIAC was the first true electronic computer, even though it had no internal memory. Von Neumann proposed storing instructions in the computer, using machine language. This breakthrough led the way for the development of EDVAC and EDSAC, both using internal memory and stored instructions.

● First-generation computers used vacuum tubes to control internal operations. These machines were very large, inaccurate, and generated a lot of heat.

● Second-generation computers relied on transistors for controlling internal operations. Transistors were much smaller, faster, and more reliable than vacuum tubes.

● Third-generation computers used solid-state integrated circuits rather than transistors to obtain reductions in size and cost together with increased reliability and speed.

● Fourth-generation computers rely on large-scale integration and continue to offer improvements in size, speed, and cost.

● The only language the computer can use directly is machine language. Symbolic languages using mnemonics make programming easier, but they have to be translated into machine language by a separate program. Higher-level languages resemble English, are easier to use than symbolic languages, and also must be translated.

● In organized information, a single data item is called a field, a collection of data items that relate to a single unit is a record, and a group of related records is a file.

● Batch processing is a method of processing data whereby transaction records are collected and sorted into a sequential order to match the sequence of the master file that is to be updated before being run through the computer.

● With direct-access processing, data can be submitted to the computer in the order it occurs. Direct-access storage devices (DASDs) allow a particular record to be accessed directly and updated without the computer having to read all preceding records on the file.

● Online processing refers to using input/output and storage devices that are in direct communication with the computer.

● The combined use of communication facilities and data-processing equipment is called teleprocessing. It allows data to be collected from widely scattered points of origin and transmitted to a central location for processing. Telephone lines, microwave transmitters, and satellites are all used in the communication of data.

● Analog transmission is sending data in wave form, whereas digital transmission sends data in pulse form. Modems are used to transfer data from digital to wave form (modulation) and back to digital form (demodulation). This conversion is required to send data through telephone channels.

● As businesses expand operations geographically, a greater demand for satellite communication systems results. With advanced technology, satellite communication is becoming a practical and efficient method of communication. However, satellites are subject to many natural phenomena, including storms, hail, rain, and fog. Precautions must be taken against war and sabotage. Transmission problems may occur because of time delays, downtime, security problems, or natural disasters.

● Under timesharing, two or more users can access the same central-computer resources and receive what seem to be simultaneous results.

REVIEW QUESTIONS

1. The first use of punched cards occurred
   a. during the 1890 census.
   b. in the weaving industry.
   c. when IBM made them.
   d. during the second generation of computers.

2. With a direct-access system, data usually will be submitted to the computer
   a. in alphabetical order.
   b. in the order that they occur.
   c. after a certain number of items have been collected.
   d. in numerical order.

3. Computers derive most of their power from what features?
   a. Input, output
   b. Storage, data, operations
   c. Intelligence, circuitry
   d. Speed, accuracy, memory

4. Second-generation computer technology consisted of
   a. integrated circuits.
   b. vacuum-tube memory.
   c. transistors.
   d. cathode-ray tubes.

5. All computer processing follows the same basic flow pattern. What is it?
   a. Input, results, transformation
   b. Input, processing, output
   c. Data, operations, output
   d. Processing, data, output

6. What is the proper term for a collection of related fields?
   a. Data base
   b. Record
   c. Data file
   d. Byte

7. Applications requiring the solution of complicated formulas with answers carried to many decimal places are referred to as
   a. machine-language applications.
   b. business applications.
   c. symbolic-language applications.
   d. scientific applications.

8. Babbage's concept of the _____ in 1833 led to the computer more than a hundred years later.
   a. analytical engine
   b. census tabulator
   c. difference engine
   d. adding machine

9. One high-level programming language is
   a. binary code.
   b. FORTRAN.
   c. symbolic language.
   d. machine language.

10. Alphabetic or numeric characters are represented in
    a. bits.
    b. bytes.
    c. fields.
    d. records.

11. Direct-access storage devices include
    a. magnetic disks.
    b. magnetic tape.
    c. punched cards.
    d. translators.

12. In _____ processing, all records in a master file must be rewritten whenever one record in the file is changed.
    a. sequential
    b. direct-access
    c. either sequential or direct-access
    d. indexed sequential

13. A key serves as a unique identifier for a
    a. field.
    b. record.
    c. character.
    d. transaction.

14. The instruction set
    a. is designed into the electronic circuitry.
    b. is input whenever the computer is programmed.
    c. is very adaptable and versatile.
    d. both b and c.

15. A collection of records containing new information waiting to be processed is known as a
    a. master file.
    b. transaction file.
    c. data base.
    d. processing file.

16. A phrase that has become fundamental to understanding computer "mistakes" is

    a. "What goes in—must come out."
    b. "Garbage in—garbage out."
    c. "The computer knows best."
    d. "People can make mistakes but to really foul things up, it takes a computer."

17. A disadvantage of direct-access processing is that

    a. records need to be sorted prior to processing.
    b. master files must be stored on tape.
    c. master files are usually not up-to-date.
    d. backup files are not automatically generated.

18. Magnetic doughnut-shaped rings composing primary storage are magnetic

    a. bubbles.
    b. rings.
    c. bits.
    d. cores.

19. A (n) _____ system can return information fast enough to affect a decision at hand.

    a. real-time
    b. on-time
    c. online
    d. inline

20. A technological process that allows circuits containing thousands of transistors to be densely packed on a single silicon chip is

    a. large-scale integration.
    b. virtual storage.
    c. modular circuits.
    d. solid-state main storage.

PART TWO

HARDWARE TECHNOLOGY

INTRODUCTION
Instructions
Memory Allocation
CPU Interaction

CPU MEMORY
Organization
Speed
Data Representation
Binary Representation
Computer Codes
Primary-Storage Technology
Read-Only Memory

COMMUNICATING WITH THE CPU
Data-Recording Media
Punched Card
Key-to-Magnetic Media
Input/Output Devices
Source-Data Automation
Printers
Special-Purpose Output
Input/Output Processors
Channels
Multiplexers and Concentrators
Programmable Communications Processors

COMPUTER SIZES AND CONFIGURATIONS
Mainframes
Supercomputers
Minicomputers
Distributed Processing
Microcomputers
Applications
Computer Stores
Networks

SUMMARY
REVIEW QUESTIONS

A basic understanding of computer hardware technology is essential in order to prepare instructions that will generate valid output. The simple diagram in Figure 2–1 reviews the principal components of a computer system.

Instructions

The real power behind any computer is the program that makes it run. Programs are called **software,** to distinguish them from the machines themselves, which are called **hardware.** A computer program is a series of instructions to be executed by the computer. These instructions can be written in any programming language but must be translated into machine language for execution. Each machine-language instruction has two basic parts: the operation code and the operand. The **operation code (op code)** tells the control unit what function is to be performed (such as ADD, SUBTRACT, MOVE DATA, or COMPARE). The **operand** indicates the primary storage location of the data to be operated on.

Memory Allocation   In early computers, instructions had to be either wired on control panels plugged into the computer or read into the computer from punched cards in discrete steps as the job progressed. The punched-card method slowed down processing because the computer had to wait for instructions to be fed in by a human operator. In later computers, instructions were stored in the computer's memory in electronic form, thus no human intervention was required during processing. This development allowed the computer to proceed at its own speed—almost the speed of light!

FIGURE 2–1 Computer System Components

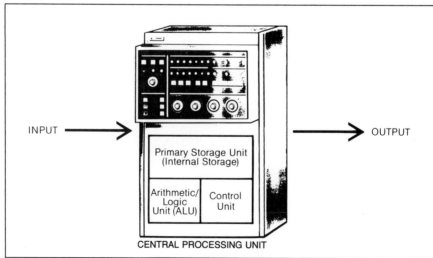

Modern computers are stored-program computers. Once the instructions required for a particular application have been determined, they are placed into the computer memory so that the appropriate operations will be performed. The storage unit operates much as a tape recorder does: Once a copy of the instructions and data has been stored, it remains in storage (on the tape) until new instructions and data are stored over them (a new recording is made). Therefore, it is possible to execute the same instructions or use the same data over and over again until a change is desired. This basic characteristic of memory is known as **nondestructive read/destructive write.** As with your tapes, "reading," or playing them does not change the content; but "writing," or recording a new message destroys the previously stored material. Each series of instructions placed into memory is called a stored program, and the person who writes these instructions is called a **programmer.**

The computer performs instructions sequentially, in the order they are given, unless instructed to do otherwise. This **next-sequential-instruction feature** requires that the instructions be placed in consecutive locations in the computer's memory. The computer simply goes from one location to the next in executing statements unless one of these instructions tells it to do otherwise. Since data must also be brought into the computer memory to be processed, a separate area must be designated for input. Otherwise, the computer would be unable to differentiate between instructions and data. This is also true for output generated by the program. Figure 2–2 shows this segmentation of memory.

CPU Interaction The three parts (control, ALU, and storage) of the central processing unit interact to process a program as follows: Initially, the control unit directs the input device to transfer instructions and data to primary storage. Then the control unit takes one instruction from storage, examines it, and sends the appropriate electronic signals to the ALU and to storage to cause the instruction to be carried out. The signals sent to storage may, for instance, tell it to transfer data to

FIGURE 2–2 Stored Program in Primary Memory

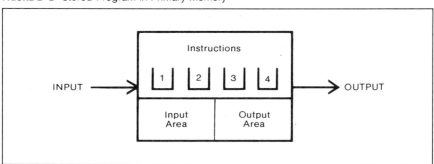

the ALU, where the data is mathematically manipulated. The result then may be transferred back to storage.

After an instruction has been executed, the control unit takes the next instruction from the primary-storage unit. Data may be transferred from storage to the ALU and back several times before all instructions are executed. When all instructions have been executed, the control unit directs the storage unit to transfer the processed data (information) to the output device.

CPU MEMORY
Organization

To accomplish such rapid processing, computers must be able to retain and, when necessary, retrieve instructions and data items. Two types of storage are present in most computer systems. Primary storage includes all storage considered part of the CPU. In computers manufactured during the 1960s and early 1970s, the most common type of primary storage was magnetic-core storage. Magnetic cores are iron-alloy doughnut-shaped rings about the size of a pinhead. Millions of these cores are strung on sections of thin wire mesh to make up the memory unit. Primary storage may be supplemented by secondary (auxiliary or external) storage, which operates under many of the same principles as primary storage, but at slower speeds. The most common types of secondary storage devices are magnetic tape and magnetic disk units.

Recall that the basic unit of storage is the bit. A bit can store one binary digit (0 or 1). The term bit comes from the first and last letters of the phrase **binary digit.** Bits, as described, are very small units of data; it is often useful to combine them into larger units. A fixed number of adjacent bits operated on as a unit is called a byte. Since eight bits are sufficient to represent any character, 8-bit groupings are the basic units of memory. In computers that accept 8-bit characters, a byte is a group of eight adjacent bits.

When large amounts of storage are described, the symbol **K** is often used as an abbreviation for **kilobyte,** which is approximately a thousand bytes. Generally, one K equals 1,024 (2^{10}) units. Thus, a computer that has 256 K bytes of storage can store 256 $\times$ 1,024 (262,144) characters. When the storage capabilities of very large computers are discussed, the term megabyte may be encountered. A **megabyte** is a million bytes.

Speed

Computers, like humans, can execute only one task at a time, but computers work remarkably fast. A new set of terms has been developed to specify the speed of these electronic devices:

millisecond = 1/1,000 second
microsecond = 1/1,000,000 second

nanosecond = 1/1,000,000,000 second
picosecond = 1/1,000,000,000,000 second

One nanosecond is a time slice so short that it is beyond the comprehension of most individuals. Light moving at a speed of 186,000 miles per second travels almost one foot in a nanosecond.

The speed at which a computer operates is dependent on the size and physical characteristics of the machine. Time requirements for performing one addition may range from four microseconds to two hundred nanoseconds. This means that a machine can do more than *one million* additions in *one second.* Obviously, such processing speed far exceeds human capabilities and is one of the principal reasons that computers are so valuable in data processing.

Data Representation

Binary Representation Data representation in the CPU is based on the presence or absence of electrical signals. Therefore, two possible states exist: Either a signal is present or it is not. This **binary system** operates in a manner similar to the decimal system.

In analyzing the decimal number 4,672, for example, we have:

4 6 7 2

$2 \times 10^0 =$ 2
$7 \times 10^1 =$ 70
$6 \times 10^2 =$ 600
$4 \times 10^3 =$ 4,000
———
4,672

or

| 4 | 6 | 7 | 2 |

10^3 10^2 10^1 10^0

Each position of the number represents a certain power of 10, and the progression of powers is from right to left.

The same principle holds for binary representation. The difference is that in binary representation each position in the number represents a power of 2. For example, consider the decimal number 14. In binary, the value equivalent to 14 is written as follows:

1 1 1 0

$0 \times 2^0 =$ 0
$1 \times 2^1 =$ 2
$1 \times 2^2 =$ 4
$1 \times 2^3 =$ 8
—
14

or

| 1 | 1 | 1 | 0 |

2^3 2^2 2^1 2^0

As you can see, the position values of a binary number are set according to the progression of powers of 2: 2^0, 2^1, 2^2, 2^3, 2^4, 2^5, and so on. A 1 in a position indicates the presence of a power of 2, whereas a

0 indicates its absence. Every binary number, regardless of magnitude, is a combination of 0s and 1s.

As a further example, the value represented by the decimal number 300 is represented in binary form as shown here:

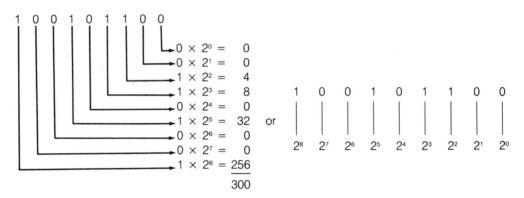

Computer Codes   Many computers use coding schemes other than simple binary notation to represent numbers. One of the most basic coding schemes is 4-bit **binary-coded decimal (BCD).** Rather than represent a decimal number as a string of 0s and 1s (which gets increasingly complicated for large numbers), BCD represents each decimal digit (0 through 9) in a number, by using four bits (Figure 2–3). For instance, the decimal number 23 is represented by two groups of four bits, one group for the "2," the other for the "3." Representations of the number 23 in 4-bit BCD and in binary are compared here:

```
0 0 1 0      0 0 1 1
|_____|    |_____|      4-bit BCD
   2            3
0000000000010111            Binary
```

The representation of a three-digit decimal number in 4-bit BCD consists of three sets of four bits, or twelve binary digits. For example, the decimal number 637 is coded as follows:

```
0 1 1 0      0 0 1 1      0 1 1 1
|_____|    |_____|    |_____|    4-bit BCD
   6            3            7
0000001001111101                       Binary
```

Use of 4-bit BCD saves space when large decimal numbers must be represented. Furthermore, it is easier to convert a 4-bit BCD to its decimal equivalent than to convert a binary representation to decimal.

The 4-bit code allows sixteen (2^4) possible unique bit combinations. We have already seen that ten of them are used to represent decimal digits 0 through 9. Since that leaves only six remaining combinations, this code is used only to represent numbers.

FIGURE 2–3 Binary-Coded Decimal

Decimal Integer	BCD Digit			
	2^3	2^2	2^1	2^0
0	0	0	0	0
1	0	0	0	1
2	0	0	1	0
3	0	0	1	1
4	0	1	0	0
5	0	1	0	1
6	0	1	1	0
7	0	1	1	1
8	1	0	0	0
9	1	0	0	1

So that the representation of alphabetic data could be achieved, an eight-digit coding system has been developed that allows 256 (2^8) possible bit combinations. Each code combination has four additional positions placed to the left, which are known as zone bits. The four bits to the far right are known as numeric bits. The zone bits are used in various combinations with numeric bits to represent numbers, letters, and special characters. The approach is similar to the construction of letters and numbers from a grouping of dots and dashes in Morse code. The coding scheme shown in Figure 2–4 is known as **Extended Binary-Coded Decimal Interchange Code (EBCDIC).**

As can be seen, numbers in a computer can be represented by using a pure binary representation or by using one of the coded-decimal representations (BCD or EBCDIC). Generally, business-oriented machines store numbers in primary memory using a coded-decimal system. However, some arithmetic operations are performed in pure binary; in such a case, the numbers used must be converted from BCD or EBCDIC to binary and back again before and after the computations. Also, not all machines use the EBCDIC coding scheme. Some computers use a 7-bit coding system known as **American Standard Code for Information Interchange (ASCII).** An 8-bit version of this code, ASCII–8, is also available for machines that are designed to use an eight-digit coding scheme. These codes are similar to EBCDIC, differing only in the bit configurations for character representation.

Code Checking. Computers do not always function perfectly; errors can and do occur. For example, a bit may be lost while data is being transferred from the ALU to the primary storage unit or over telephone lines from one location to another. This loss can be caused by dust, moisture, magnetic fields, equipment failure, or other things. Thus, it is necessary

FIGURE 2–4 EBCDIC Representation: 0–9, A–Z

Character	EBCDIC Zone	EBCDIC Numeric	Character	EBCDIC Zone	EBCDIC Numeric
A	1100	0001	S	1110	0010
B	1100	0010	T	1110	0011
C	1100	0011	U	1110	0100
D	1100	0100	V	1110	0101
E	1100	0101	W	1110	0110
F	1100	0110	X	1110	0111
G	1100	0111	Y	1110	1000
H	1100	1000	Z	1110	1001
I	1100	1001	0	1111	0000
J	1101	0001	1	1111	0001
K	1101	0010	2	1111	0010
L	1101	0011	3	1111	0011
M	1101	0100	4	1111	0100
N	1101	0101	5	1111	0101
O	1101	0110	6	1111	0110
P	1101	0111	7	1111	0111
Q	1101	1000	8	1111	1000
R	1101	1001	9	1111	1001

to have a method to detect when an error has occurred and to isolate the location of the error.

So that this task can be accomplished, most computers have at each storage location an additional bit, called a **parity bit,** or **check bit.** Computers that use parity bits are specifically designed to always have either an even or an odd number of 1-bits (or "on" bits) in each storage location. Regardless of the type of code used, if an odd number of 1-bits is used to represent each character, the characters are said to be written in **odd parity.** Similarly, if an even number of 1-bits is used to represent each character, the characters are written in **even parity.** Internal circuitry in the computer constantly monitors its operation by checking to ensure that the required number of bits is present in each location.

For example, if BCD code is used, a fifth bit is added as a check bit. Suppose the number 7 is to be represented in BCD using even parity (Figure 2–5). In this case, the check bit must be set to 1, or "on," to make the number of 1-bits even. If a parity error is detected, the system may retry the read or write operation occurring when the error was detected. If retries are unsuccessful, the system informs the computer operator that an error has occurred.

Notice that the checking circuitry of the computer can only detect the miscoding of characters. It cannot detect the use of incorrect data. In the previous example, for instance, the computer circuitry could determine whether a bit had been dropped, making the representation of the number 6 invalid. However, if the number 5 had been mistakenly

FIGURE 2–5 Detection of Error with Parity Check (Even Parity)

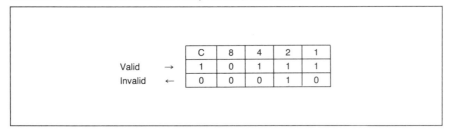

		C	8	4	2	1
Valid	→	1	0	1	1	1
Invalid	←	0	0	0	1	0

entered into the computer instead of 6 (say, because of incorrect keying of a card), no error would have been detected.

Primary-Storage Technology

Some primary-storage units are composed of magnetic cores. Magnetic-core memory operates on the principle of a magnetic field being created when electricity flows through a wire **(Gauss's law).** Each core operates in a binary mode in that the core can be magnetized in either a clockwise or counterclockwise manner. Thus, each core can hold one bit of information. A clockwise magnetization represents a 0. Only half the current needed to magnetize a core is sent through each of the two wires intersecting within a particular core (Figure 2–6). Thus, only where the wires intersect will the current be strong enough to magnetize a core. The desired core is magnetized while neighboring cores remain unaffected. If the polarity of the magnetization is reversed, the direction of the current flow in the wires is reversed.

In most computers manufactured since the mid–1970s, the primary-storage unit consists of semiconductor-storage components. **Semiconductor memory**, *also called* **random access memory (RAM)**, uses tiny integrated circuits etched on thin silicon chips. These circuits consist of thousands of storage cells. Each cell contains a transistor, which serves as an electronic switch, and a capacitor, which is capable of storing a small electrical charge. When the capacitor is off—that is, when it holds no charge—a "0" state exists. When the capacitor is turned on—when it holds a charge—a "1" state exists. Thus, the circuits operate in a binary mode through the presence or absence of electrical charges in the storage cells. The transistor in each cell functions to turn each cell on or off. The control unit of the CPU "reads" the memory by testing the electrical contents of each cell in the circuit.

Semiconductor-storage units have replaced magnetic-core units for several reasons. First, semiconductors are much less bulky than magnetic cores. A given volume of storage, in bits, will take up much less space in semiconductor storage than in core storage. Second, semiconductor units operate much faster than core units. Finally, the point has

FIGURE 2–6 Selecting a Core

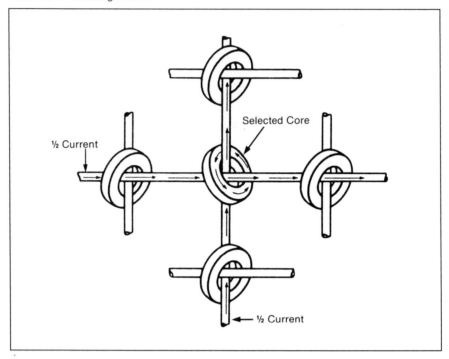

recently been reached where both manufacturing and owning semiconductor storage have become less expensive than core storage on a per-
bit basis. However, semiconductor storage has one serious drawback.
Since information is stored using currents, a constant power source is
needed to ensure that no data is lost. If the power source to the semiconductor unit is interrupted, even for a fraction of a second, all data
stored in the unit will be lost. Storage of this nature is said to be **volatile.**
In contrast, core storage, since it operates on magnetism, is nonvolatile;
it maintains its contents even in the event of a power failure. Many
organizations using semiconductor storage maintain a·backup power
system so that a steady power supply can be ensured for their machines.

A device called **bubble memory** was introduced as a replacement
medium not only for primary storage but also for auxiliary storage. This
memory consists of magnetized spots (or bubbles) resting on a thin film
of semiconductor material having polarity opposite that of the semiconductor material on which they rest. Data is stored by shifting the
bubbles' positions on the surface of the material. When data is read,
the presence of a bubble indicates a 0 bit. The bubbles are similar to
magnetic cores in that they retain their magnetism indefinitely. Bubbles
are much smaller than magnetic cores, but more data can be stored in
this smaller area. A bubble-memory module only slightly larger than a
quarter can store 20,000 characters of data.

Some manufacturers have introduced bubble memory in computers; however, a more common use of bubble memories is to provide limited storage capabilities in input/output devices. High cost and difficulty of production have been major factors limiting wide industry and user acceptance of bubbles.

Read-Only Memory

Computers are capable of performing complex functions, such as taking square roots and evaluating exponents. Such functions can be built into either the hardware or the software (the programs) of a computer system. Building them into the hardware provides the advantages of speed and reliability, since the operations are part of the actual computer circuitry. Building them into software allows more flexibility, but carrying out functions built into software is slower and more prone to error.

When functions are built into the hardware of a computer, they are placed in **read-only memory (ROM).** Read-only memory instructions are **hardwired;** that is, they cannot be changed or deleted by other stored-program instructions. Since ROM is permanent, it cannot be occupied by common stored-program instructions or data. The only method of changing its contents is by altering the physical construction of the circuits.

A direct result of this characteristic is **microprogramming.** Microprograms are sequences of instructions built into read-only memory to carry out functions (such as calculating square roots) that otherwise would have to be directed by stored-program instructions at a much slower speed. Microprograms are usually supplied by computer manufacturers and cannot be altered by users. However, microprogramming allows the basic operations of the computer to be tailored to meet the needs of users. If all instructions that a computer can execute are located in ROM, a new set of instructions can be obtained by changing the ROM chip. When selecting a computer, users can get the standard features of the machine plus their choice of the optional features available through microprogramming. Many minicomputers and microcomputers today are directed by instructions stored in ROM. Note that the concept of read-only memory differs from the concept of nondestructive read. The contents of regular primary memory can be read repeatedly without a loss of data, but these contents can be altered through conventional programming instructions. The contents of ROM cannot be changed in this manner.

Recently, a new version of ROM that can be programmed by the end user has been made available. This memory is known as **programmable read-only memory (PROM).** PROM can be programmed by the manufacturer, or it can be shipped "blank" to the end user, who can personally program it. Once programmed, the contents of PROM are unalterable. Thus, PROM is memory that can be programmed through conventional methods, but only one time. PROM enables the end user to have the advantages of ROM along with the flexibility to meet unique needs. A problem with PROM, though, is that mistakes programmed into the unit cannot be corrected. So that this drawback could be overcome, **erasable programmable read-only memory (EPROM)** has been developed. EPROM can be erased, but only by submitting the memory unit to a special process, such as bathing the unit in ultraviolet light.

COMMUNICATING WITH THE CPU
Data-Recording Media

Punched Card   The oldest medium for entering data into a computer system is the punched card. The standard punched card has eighty vertical columns and twelve horizontal rows. It is capable of holding eighty characters of data in the form of numbers, letters, and special characters. An individual data character is represented by the presence or absence of punched holes in the rows within one card column (Figure 2–7).

Horizontally, the card is organized into three sections. There are ten number rows in a column, and they can be used to represent any digit, 0 through 9. Two zone rows are immediately above the number rows. The zone rows are used in combination with the number rows to represent letters and special characters. The third section is at the very top of the card. It can be used to display what is punched into the card in a form that is easily readable by humans.

Data is most commonly recorded on punched cards with the use of a **keypunch.** Keypunching can be quite costly. One person is needed to operate each keypunch machine, and much time is spent keying data.

FIGURE 2–7 Eighty-Column Punched Card and Hollerith Code

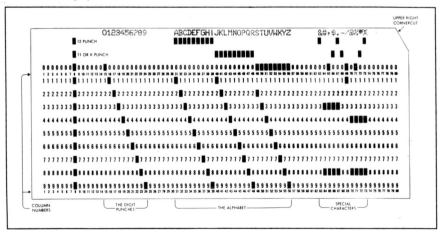

Each punched card is a **unit record**—a complete record of one set of information. For instance, a card that represents the sale of an item may include the part number, the quantity purchased, and the date of sale. Unit records can be added, sorted, or deleted by merely removing cards or contributing cards to a deck of related records. This deck would be called a file. Cards have a low cost; however, they are bulky to store and must be protected from mutilation. If a unit record requires fewer than eighty columns, the remaining space on the card is unused and thus wasted.

Card readers are the devices that read punched cards. The card readers in use today are constructed in one of two ways (Figure 2–8). The first type of card reader uses metal brushes to determine the positions of the holes in a card column. As the brushes pass over a hole, they complete an electrical circuit. This process automatically translates the presence or absence of holes into a set of electrical pulses.

The **photoelectric card reader** is another type of card reader available. Instead of brushes, a light source is used. As light passes through the holes in a card, it activates a photoelectric cell behind the card. This completes an electrical circuit, and an appropriate electrical signal is transmitted. Photoelectric readers are more reliable than brush-type readers since they are not dependent on metal brushes, which can be damaged easily.

Key-to-Magnetic Media Punched-card systems require much mechanized movement and have many limitations. New methods have been developed to record and enter data using magnetic media, such as magnetic tape or magnetic disks, rather than cards. Data is entered in much the same fashion as with the keypunch, but it is stored not as punches but as magnetized spots on the surface of a tape or disk. As a result of advancing technology, most **key-to-tape** systems will eventually be replaced by systems using disks or diskettes. A typical **key-to-disk** config-

FIGURE 2–8 Card-Reading Methods

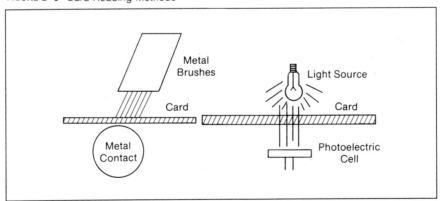

uration consists of several keying devices, all of which are connected to a minicomputer. Data is usually edited by the minicomputer and then recorded onto magnetic disks (Figure 2–9). The editing is directed by the minicomputer's stored-program instructions. If an error is detected, the system interrupts the operator and "stands by" until a correction has been entered. The correct data is then stored on the magnetic disk for input to the computer. An increasingly popular data-entry system is the **key-to-diskette system.** A flexible (or floppy) diskette is used instead of the conventional hard disk. The data is entered on a keyboard, displayed on a screen for the operator to check, and recorded on the diskette. A key-to-diskette system can operate by itself or with a group of similar devices.

Magnetic Tape. A magnetic tape is a continuous plastic strip wound on a reel, quite similar to the tape used in reel-to-reel stereo recorders. The magnetic tape's plastic base is treated with a magnetizable coating. Typically, the tape is one-half inch in width. It is wound in lengths of 2,400 feet on ten-and-one-half-inch-diameter reels. Magnetic tapes are also packaged in cartridges for use with small computers.

Data is stored on magnetic tape by magnetizing small spots of the iron-oxide coating on the tape. Although these spots can be read by the computer, they are invisible to the human eye. Large volumes of information can be stored on a single tape; densities of 1,600 characters per

FIGURE 2–9 Key-to-Disk System

inch are common, and some tapes are capable of storing up to 6,250 characters per inch. A typical reel of 2,400 feet can store as much as 400,000 punched cards.

A magnetic tape is mounted on a **tape drive** when the information it contains is needed by a program (Figure 2–10). The tape drive has a **read/write head** (actually an electromagnet) that creates or reads the bits as the tape moves past it (Figure 2–11). When it is reading, the read/write head detects the magnetized areas and converts them into electrical pulses to send to the CPU. When writing, the head magnetizes the appropriate spots on the tape, erasing any previously stored data. Thus, writing is destructive and reading is nondestructive.

Individual records on magnetic tape are separated by **interrecord gaps (IRGs)** (Figure 2–12). These gaps do not contain data but perform

FIGURE 2–10 Magnetic-Tape Drive

FIGURE 2–11 Recording on Magnetic Tape

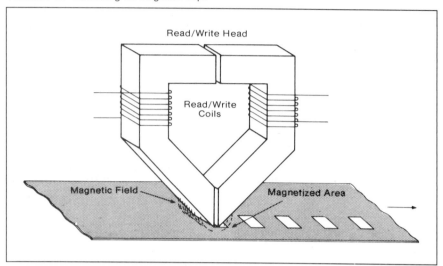

another function. A tape is rarely read in its entirety, all at once. Rather, it is stopped after the end of a record is reached. The tape must then be accelerated to the correct speed to allow the next record to be read correctly; otherwise, the result would be similar to what happens when a phonograph record is played at the wrong speed. The IRG allows the tape to regain the proper speed before the next record is read. The length of the interrecord gap depends on the speed of the tape drive; if the tape drive is very fast, longer gaps are needed, whereas slower speeds require shorter gaps.

If records are very short and divided by equally long IRGs, the tape may be more than 50 percent blank, causing the tape drive to be constantly stopping and accelerating. So that this possibility can be avoided, records may be grouped, or blocked. These **blocked records, or blocks,** are separated by **interblock gaps (IBGs)** (Figure 2–13). Now instead of

FIGURE 2–12 Magnetic-Tape Records

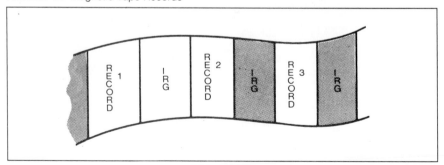

FIGURE 2-13 Blocked Records

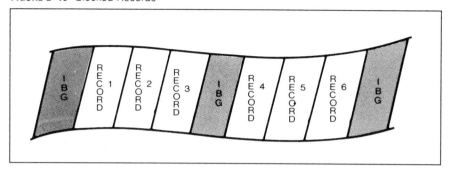

reading a short record and accelerating past blank tape, reading a short record and accelerating, and so on, the read/write head reads a block of records before it needs to skip blank portions of tape. This method reduces the overall input/output time. An entire block of records can be transferred at one time to primary storage for processing. Blocking also reduces the wasted space on the tape, permitting more records to be stored on a given length of tape.

Small computer systems may not need a large amount of auxiliary storage. For these systems, **tape cassettes** have been developed. Tape cassettes look like those used in audio recording, and some may even be used with a typical cassette player/recorder. The major difference between the two types of tape cassettes is the tape: Tape cassettes used for storing data use higher-quality, high-density, digital recording tape.

Because of the low cost and convenience of tape cassettes, their use for input, output, and storage has increased greatly in minicomputer and microcomputer systems. Tape cassettes are an ideal storage system for home computers. They can be used with a standard cassette player. Tape cassettes are easy to store and also provide security, since they can be removed from the system and carried with the user. The major disadvantage of cassettes is that they are a sequential medium. To locate a particular spot, you must search the length of the tape. This can be slow and irritating at times.

Magnetic Disk.   The conventional magnetic disk is a metal platter fourteen inches in diameter, coated on both sides with a magnetizable material like iron oxide. In many respects, a magnetic disk resembles a phonograph record. However, it does not have a phonograph record's characteristic grooves; its surfaces are smooth. Nevertheless, a disk unit does store and retrieve data in much the same fashion as a phonograph. The disk is rotated while a read/write head is positioned above its magnetic surface. Instead of spiraling in to the center of the disk like the needle of a phonograph, however, the data is stored in a set of concentric circles. Each circle is referred to as a **track.** One track never touches another, as shown in Figure 2–14. A typical disk has two hundred tracks per surface.

FIGURE 2–14 Top View of Disk Surface Showing Concentric Tracks

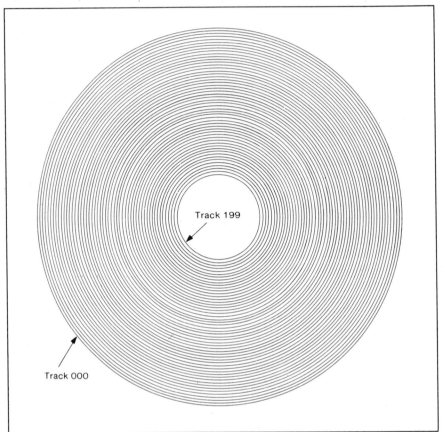

In most disk-storage devices, several disks are assembled to form a **disk pack** (Figure 2–15) and mounted on a center shaft. The individual disks are spaced on the shaft to allow room for a mechanism to move between them (Figure 2–16). The disk pack in Figure 2–16 has eleven disks and provides twenty usable recording surfaces; the top and bottom surfaces are not used for storing data because they are likely to become scratched or nicked. A disk pack may contain anywhere from six to eleven disks.

A disk pack must be positioned in a disk drive when the data on the pack is to be processed. The **disk drive** rotates all disks in unison, at a speed ranging from 40 to 3,600 revolutions per second. In some models, the disk packs are removable; in others, the disks are permanently mounted on the disk drive. Removable disk packs allow disk files to be removed when the data they contain is not needed. Users of removable disk packs typically have many more disk packs than disk drives.

FIGURE 2–15 Disk Pack

The data on a disk is read or written by the read/write heads between the disks. Most disk units have one read/write head for each disk-recording surface. All the heads are permanently connected to an **access mechanism.** When reading or writing occurs, the heads are positioned over the appropriate track by the in-and-out movement of the access mechanism (Figure 2–16). Some disk units have one read/write head for each track. The access time is much faster with this type of disk unit, since the access mechanism does not need to move from track to track. These units are more expensive.

Because disks provide direct access, they are typically used to store data against which frequent inquiries are required. Transfer rates of up to 850,000 characters per second are possible, depending on the disk drive.

The **flexible disk, diskette, or floppy disk** (Figure 2–17) was introduced in 1973 to replace punched cards as a medium for data entry, but it can also store programs and data files. These floppy disks are made of plastic, and coated with an oxide substance. They are, in most respects, miniature magnetic disks. The diskettes often sell for as little as $2.50 and are very popular for use with micro- and minicomputer systems and point-of-sale terminals. They are reusable, easy to store, and weigh less than two ounces. They are readily interchangeable and can even be mailed. Because flexible disks are removable, they provide added security for a computer system. A typical disk can store as much

FIGURE 2–16 Disk Pack Showing Read/Write Heads

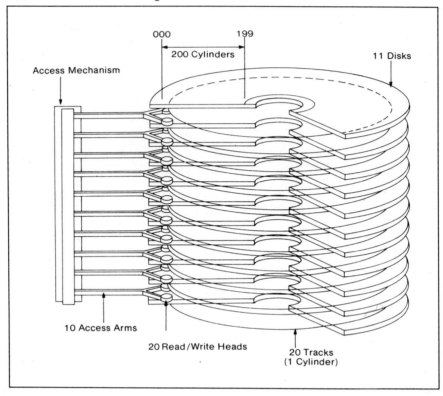

as 3,000 punched cards. Advances in technology are greatly expanding the floppy disk's storage capacity.

Input/Output Devices

The media just described—cards, tape, and disks—are very versatile. They can be used for input, storage, or output purposes. Other communication devices are more specialized.

Source-Data Automation Data entry has traditionally been the weakest link in the chain of data-processing operations. Although data can be processed electronically at extremely high speeds, significantly more time is required to prepare data and enter it into the computer system.

Consider a computer system that uses punched cards for data input. The data is first written on some type of coding form or source document. Then it is keypunched onto cards by an operator. Next, the keypunched data may be checked for accuracy, a process called **verification,** by duplicating the entire keypunching operation. Incorrect cards must be keypunched and verified a second time. After all data has been recorded

FIGURE 2–17 Floppy Disk

correctly on cards, other operations may be required before the cards are read into the computer. For instance, card files may be copied onto magnetic tape for later input to the computer because magnetic-tape files can be read into the computer much faster than card files.

This method of entering data into the computer is time-consuming and expensive. Some organizations have turned to the key-to-tape, key-to-disk, or key-to-diskette systems just described, to simplify keying operations. Another approach to data collection and preparation is also gaining popularity; it is called **source-data automation.** The purpose of source-data automation is to collect data about an event, in computer-readable form, when and where the event takes place. Because the intermediate steps used in preparing card input are eliminated, source-data automation improves the speed, accuracy, and efficiency of data-processing operations.

Source-data automation is implemented by a variety of methods. Each requires special machines for reading data and converting it into machine language. Here the most common approaches to source-data automation are discussed.

Magnetic-Ink Character Recognition. **Magnetic ink** was introduced in the late 1950s to facilitate check processing by the banking industry. Because magnetic-ink characters can be read by both humans and machines, no special data-conversion step is needed. Magnetic-ink characters are formed with magnetized particles of iron oxide. Each char-

FIGURE 2–18a Matrix Patterns for Magnetic-Ink Characters

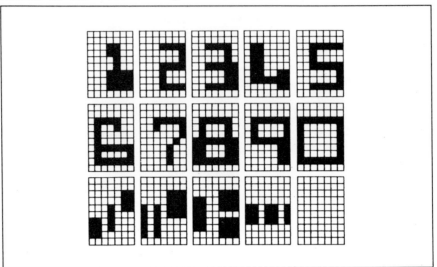

acter is composed of certain sections of a seventy-section matrix (Figure 2–18a). The characters can be read and interpreted by a **magnetic-ink character reader;** this process is called **magnetic-ink character recognition (MICR).**

All magnetic-ink characters on checks are formed with the standard fourteen-character set shown in Figure 2–18b. (Other character sets may be used in other applications.) As the checks are fed into the MICR device, it reads and sorts them by bank number at a Federal Reserve Bank and by account number at the issuing bank. In this manner, checks are routed back to each issuing bank and then back to its customers. Between 750 and 1,500 checks per minute can be read and sorted by the MICR system.

Optical Recognition. **Optical-recognition devices** can read marks or symbols coded on paper documents and convert them into electrical pulses. The pulses can then be transmitted directly to the CPU or stored on magnetic tape for input at a later time.

The simplest approach to optical recognition is known as **optical-mark recognition (OMR),** or mark-sensing. This approach is often used for machine scoring of multiple-choice examinations, where a person taking the test makes a mark with a heavy lead pencil in the location corresponding to each desired answer. The marks on an OMR document are sensed by an **optical-mark page reader** as the document passes under a light source. The presence of marks in specific locations is indicated by light reflected at those locations. As the document is read, the optical-mark data is translated into machine language. When the optical-mark

FIGURE 2–18b Magnetic-Ink Character Set

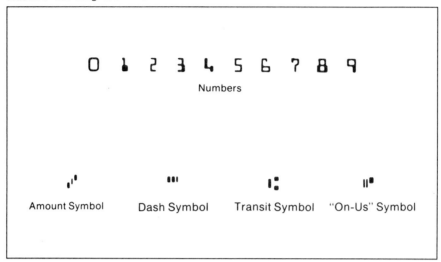

page reader is directly connected to the computer, up to 2,000 forms of the same type can be read and processed in an hour.

Another type of optical reader, known as a **bar-code reader,** can read special line, or bar, codes—patterns of optical marks. Some bar codes in use today are shown in Figure 2–19. They are suitable for many applications, including point-of-sale (POS) systems, credit-card verification, and freight identification to facilitate warehouse operations.

Data is represented in a bar code by the widths of the bars and the distances between them. Probably the most familiar bar code is the **Universal Product Code (UPC)** found on most grocery items. This code consists of ten pairs of vertical bars that represent both the manufacturer's identity and the identity of the item, but not the item's price. The code for each product is a unique combination of these vertical bars.

Optical-character readers can read special types of characters known as **optical characters.** Some **optical-character recognition (OCR)** devices can read characters of several type styles, including both uppercase and lowercase letters.

A major difference between optical-character recognition and optical-mark recognition is that optical-character data is represented by the shapes of characters rather than by the positions of marks. However, both OCR and OMR devices rely on reflected light to translate written data into machine-readable form.

Remote Input. Remote terminals collect data at its source and transmit it to a central computer for processing (online). Generally, data is transmitted over telecommunication equipment. The many types of remote

FIGURE 2–19 Types of Bar Codes

terminals available can increase the versatility and expand the applications of the computer. Types of remote terminals to be discussed here are point-of-sale terminals, touch-tone devices, voice-recognition devices, and intelligent terminals.

Remote terminals that perform the functions of a cash register and also capture sales data are referred to as **point-of-sale (POS) terminals.** Such terminals have a keyboard for data entry, a panel to display the price, a cash drawer, and a printer that provides a cash receipt.

Some POS terminals have a **wand reader** or a **fixed scanner** that reads the Universal Product Code stamped on an item. The sale is registered automatically as the checkout person passes the wand reader over the code; there is no need to enter the price via the keyboard unless the wand malfunctions. Using the UPC symbol, the computer system identifies the product and finds the item's name and price. Thus, POS terminals enable sales data to be collected at its source. If the terminals are directly connected to a large central computer, useful inventory and sales information can be provided instantaneously to the retailer.

Touch-tone devices are remote terminals used together with ordinary telephone lines to transfer data from remote locations to a central computer. The data is entered via a special keyboard on the terminal. Generally, slight modifications must be made to the telephone connection to allow data to be transferred over the line (Figure 2–20).

Remote terminals that use audio input or **voice-recognition systems** are suitable for low-volume, highly formal, input. Instead of entering data into the computer by punching keys on a terminal, the user may "train" the computer to understand his or her voice. Here, the user must follow only the patterns the computer is programmed to recognize. Computer audio output or **voice-response units** "speak" by arranging half-second recordings of voice sounds (phonemes) or prerecorded words. This approach is being used in the banking industry to report customer account balances and in supermarkets to notify customers of the amount of each purchase. Often the audio-response units are coupled with touch-tone terminals for remote data entry. An entire unit may weigh less than ten pounds, and some are built into briefcases for easy portability.

FIGURE 2–20 Touch-Tone Device

Intelligent terminals, still another type of remote device, can be programmed by use of stored instructions. This capability distinguishes them from other terminals (sometimes called **dumb terminals**), which cannot be programmed. Intelligent terminals have the same kinds of components as full-sized computers but are limited in their storage capability and in the set of instructions they can perform. They are useful for editing data prior to transmitting the data to a central computer. Editing and other manipulating functions are directed by programs stored in the terminal's primary-storage unit. Most intelligent terminals have a **CRT (cathode-ray tube)** and a printer built into them.

Printers Computer **printers** serve a straightforward basic function—printing processed data in a form humans can read (Figure 2–21). This permanent readable copy of computer output is often referred to as **hard copy.** To produce it, the printer first receives electronic signals from the central processing unit. In an **impact printer,** these signals activate print elements that are pressed against paper. **Nonimpact printers,** a newer development, use heat, laser technology, or photographic techniques to print output.

Impact Printers.   Impact printers come in a variety of shapes and sizes. Some print a character at a time whereas others print a line at a time. Printer-keyboard, wire-matrix, and daisy-wheel printers are the three principal character-at-a-time devices.

FIGURE 2–21 Printer

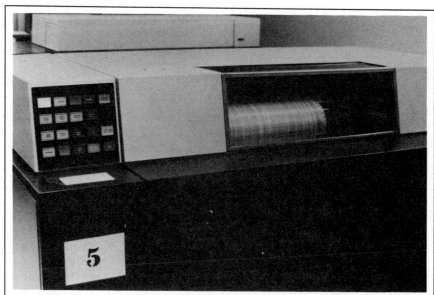

The **printer-keyboard** is similar to an office typewriter. All instructions, including spacing, carriage returns, and printing of characters, are sent from the CPU to the printers. The keyboard allows an operator to communicate with the system—for example, to enter data or instructions.

Wire-matrix (also called **dot-matrix**) **printers** are based on a design principle similar to that of a football or basketball scoreboard. The matrix is a rectangle composed of pins; usually it is seven pins high and five pins wide. Certain combinations of pins are activated and pressed against paper to represent characters. The dot combinations used to represent various numbers, letters, and special characters are shown in Figure 2–22. Wire-matrix printers typically print up to 900 characters per minute.

Daisy-wheel printers resemble office typewriters. The daisy wheel itself is a flat disk with petal-like projections (Figure 2–23). The wheel has a set of spokes, each with a single character embossed at the tip. The desired character is rotated into position and is then struck by a hammer mechanism to form an image on paper. Daisy wheels come in several type styles that can be interchanged quickly to suit application needs. The daisy-wheel printer offers high-quality type and is often used on word processors to give output a professionally typed appearance. They can produce up to fifty characters per second.

Types of line-at-a-time printers include print-wheel printers, chain printers, and drum printers. A **print-wheel printer** typically contains 132 print wheels, one for each of 132 print positions on a line (Figure 2–24). Each print wheel contains forty-eight characters, including alphabetic, numeric, and special characters. Each print wheel rotates until the desired character moves into the corresponding print position on the current print line. When all wheels are in their correct positions, a hammer drives the paper against the wheels and an entire line of

FIGURE 2–22 Wire-Matrix-Printer Character Set

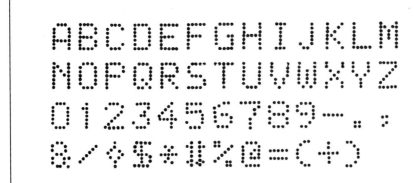

FIGURE 2–23 Daisy Wheel

output is printed. Print-wheel printers can produce about 150 lines per minute.

A **chain printer** has a character set assembled in a chain that revolves horizontally past all print positions (Figure 2–25). There is one print hammer for each column on the paper. Characters are printed when the hammers press the paper against an inked ribbon, which in turn presses against appropriate characters on the print chain. Type styles can be changed easily on chain printers, allowing a variety, such as italic or boldface, to be used. Some chain printers can produce up to 2,000 lines per minute.

A **drum printer** uses a metal cylinder with rows of characters engraved across its surface (Figure 2–26). Each column on the drum contains a complete character set and corresponds to one print position on the line. As the drum rotates, all characters are rotated past the print position. A hammer presses the paper against an ink ribbon and the drum when the appropriate character is in place. One line is printed for each revolution of the drum, since all characters eventually reach the print position during one revolution. Some drum printers can produce 3,000 lines per minute.

Nonimpact Printers. As mentioned earlier, nonimpact printers do not print characters by means of a mechanical printing element that strikes paper. Instead, a variety of other methods is used. Electrostatic, electrothermal, ink-jet, laser, and xerographic printers will be discussed here.

FIGURE 2–24 Print Wheel

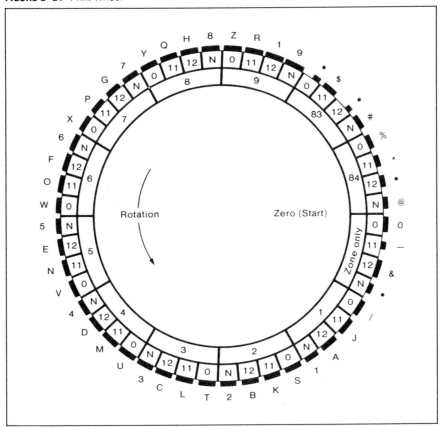

An **electrostatic printer** forms an image of a character on special paper, using a dot matrix of charged wires or pins. The paper is moved through a solution containing ink particles that have a charge opposite that of the images. The ink particles adhere to each charged pattern on the paper, forming a visible image of each character.

Electrothermal printers generate characters by using heat and heat-sensitive paper. Rods are heated in a matrix; as the ends of the selected rods touch the heat-sensitive paper, an image is created.

Both electrothermal and electrostatic printers are relatively quiet in operation. They are often used in applications where noise may be a problem. Some of these printers are capable of producing 5,000 lines per minute.

In an **ink-jet printer,** a nozzle is used to shoot a stream of charged ink toward the paper. Before reaching the paper, the ink passes through an electrical field that arranges the charged particles into characters. These printers can print 200 characters per second.

Laser printers combine laser beams and electrophotographic technology to create output images. A beam of light is focused through a

FIGURE 2–25 Chain Printer

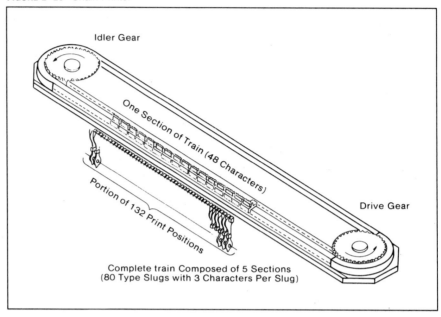

Idler Gear

One Section of Train (48 Characters)

Portion of 132 Print Positions

Drive Gear

Complete train Composed of 5 Sections
(80 Type Slugs with 3 Characters Per Slug)

rotating disk containing a full assortment of characters. The character image is projected onto a piece of film or photographic paper, and the print or negative is developed and fixed in a manner similar to that used for ordinary photographs. The output consists of high-quality, letter-perfect images—this process is often used to print books. Laser printers, which can operate up to 21,000 lines per minute, are being considered as a solution to the slower current speeds of word processing printers.

Xerographic printers use printing methods much like those used in common xerographic copying machines. For example, Xerox, the pioneer of this type of printing, has one model that prints on single 8½-by-11-inch sheets of plain paper. Xerographic printers operate at 4,000 lines per minute.

Table 2–1 shows representative differences in print speeds of impact and nonimpact printers. Since nonimpact printers involve much less physical movement than impact printers, they are generally much faster. They also offer a wider choice of type faces and better speed-to-price ratios than impact printers, and their technology implies a higher reliability because they use fewer movable parts in printing. The disadvantages of using nonimpact printers include their inability to make carbon copies, and the special paper some require. However, they can make multiple printings of a page in less time than it takes an impact printer to make one multicarbon page.

New printing systems now being introduced combine many features of the printing process into one machine. For example, collating, rout-

FIGURE 2–26 Print Drum

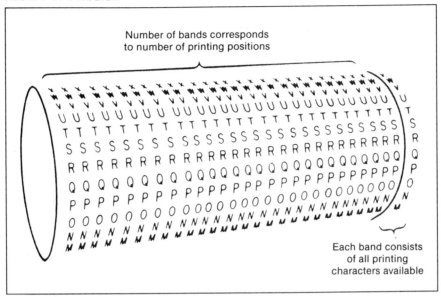

Number of bands corresponds
to number of printing positions

Each band consists
of all printing
characters available

ing, holepunching, blanking out of proprietary information, and per-
forating may be performed. Some printers produce both text and form
designs on plain paper; this reduces or eliminates the need for pre-
printed forms.

Special-Purpose Output In many instances, traditional printers cannot provide certain forms of output. At these times, special output devices are required.

Visual-Display Terminals. **Visual-display terminals** in common use display data on cathode-ray tubes (CRTs). A typical screen can hold twenty-
four lines, each containing eighty characters (some of the newer terminals have twenty-five lines, one reserved for special messages). These
terminals supply what is known as **soft-copy** output; that is, the screen
is not a permanent record of what is shown. They are well-suited for
applications involving inquiry and response where no permanent (printed)
records are required, and can be used for capturing data to be transmitted from remote offices to a central computer. Data may be entered
using a keyboard on the terminal and displayed on the screen for verification as it is keyed.

Visual-display terminals have some advantages over printers. First,
they can display output much faster than printers—some CRT terminals
can display up to 10,000 characters in a second. Also, they are much
quieter in operation than impact printers. It is usually possible to con-
nect a printer or a copier to a CRT terminal; thus, hard-copy output of
the screen contents can be provided. These terminals are rapidly gaining
recognition as desirable components of information systems.

TABLE 2–1 Printer Types and Speeds

PRINTER TYPE	PRINTING CAPABILITY
IMPACT PRINTERS	
Character-at-a-Time:	
Daisy Wheel	50 characters per second
Printer-Keyboards	900 characters per minute
Wire-Matrix (Dot-Matrix)	900 characters per minute
Line-at-a-Time:	
Print Wheel	150 lines per minute
Print Chain	2000 lines per minute
Print Drum	3000 lines per minute
NONIMPACT PRINTERS	
Ink Jet	200 characters per second
Xerographic	4000 lines per minute
Electrothermal	5000 lines per minute
Electrostatic	5000 lines per minute
Laser	21,000 lines per minute

Another type of CRT, known as a **graphic-display device,** is used to display drawings as well as characters on a screen (Figure 2–27). Graphic-display devices are generally used to display graphs and charts, but they can also show complex curves and shapes. With some terminals, data displayed on the screen can be altered by using the **light pen,** a pen-shaped object with a light-sensitive cell at its end (Figure 2–28). Users can "draw" lines on the screen by specifying the ends of the lines with the light pen and can quickly alter graphs and line drawings by applying the pen at the appropriate locations on the screen. Graphic-display devices are being used in highly technical fields, such as in the aerospace industry to aid in the design of new wing structures.

Plotters.   A **plotter** is an output device that converts data from the CPU into graphic form. It can produce lines, curves, and complex shapes. The major difference between a plotter and a graphic-display device is that the plotter produces hard-copy output (paper), whereas the graphic-display device produces soft-copy output (screen image).

A typical plotter has a pen, movable carriage, drum, and chartpaper holder (Figure 2–29). Shapes are produced as the pen moves back and forth across the paper along the y-axis while the drum moves the paper up and down along the x-axis. Both the paper movement and the pen movement are bidirectional. The pen is raised and lowered from the paper surface automatically.

The plotter can be used to produce line and bar charts, graphs, organizational charts, engineering drawings, maps, trend lines, supply

FIGURE 2–27 Graphic-Display Device

and demand curves, and so on. The figures are drawn precisely, because the pen can be positioned at as many as 45,000 points in each square inch of paper. Some plotters can produce drawings in up to eight colors. The usefulness of the plotter lies in its ability to communicate information in easy-to-understand picture form.

Computer-Output Microfilm. In situations where large volumes of information must be printed and stored for future reference, conventional paper output is not appropriate. It uses much storage space, and particular items are often difficult to locate. A possible alternative is **computer-output microfilm (COM),** which consists of photographed images produced in miniature by the computer. In some cases, the output is first recorded on magnetic tape. Special photocopying equipment is then used to reproduce the information on microfilm. In an interactive environment, the COM equipment is used to display output on a CRT screen, then the screen is exposed to microfilm. The microfilm copy can be produced as a roll of film or a four-by-six-inch microfiche card. In such a system, the speed of recording can be twenty-five to fifty times faster than traditional printing methods.

The main advantage of COM is that much data can be stored compactly, reducing both space requirements and storage costs. Also, both character and graphic output can be recorded. The use of a transparent overlay permits headings to be printed and lines superimposed so that output is highly readable. The cost of producing additional microfilm

FIGURE 2–28 Visual-Display Device with Light Pen

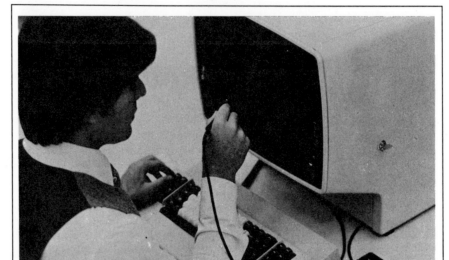

copies is very low. In the past, high initial investment costs and the inability of the computer to directly retrieve microfilmed data have been disadvantages. However, costs are declining and the number of COM systems in use is increasing.

Input/Output Processors

Channels Although the central processing unit (CPU) is very fast and accurate, it can execute only one instruction at a time. If the CPU is executing an instruction that indicates an input or output operation, it must wait until that operation is completed before it can continue. Compared with internal CPU speed, input/output speeds are extremely slow. Even high-speed input/output devices often work only one-tenth as fast as the central processing unit. When the CPU is slowed down because of input/output operations, the system is said to be **input/output bound.**

So that such problems could be avoided, **channels** were developed. Channels take over the task of input and output from the CPU. It may be within the CPU or be a separate piece of equipment connected to the CPU. Each channel serves as a data roadway upon command of the CPU to handle the slow-speed input/output operations. This relieves the CPU of its responsibility for data transfer (and therefore its need to wait).

FIGURE 2-29 Desktop Plotter

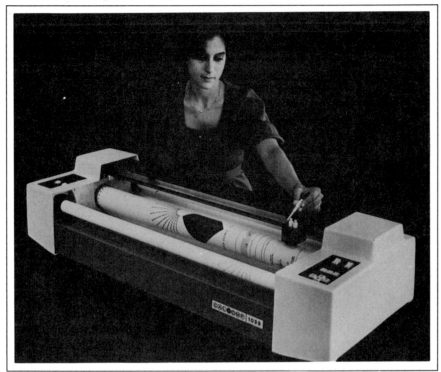

Multiplexers and Concentrators **Multiplexers** and **concentrators** increase the number of devices that can use a communication channel. Terminals operate at a much slower speed (100 to 150 bits per second) than do communication channels (300 to 9,600 bits per second for voice grade). Thus, a channel is not used to full capacity by a single terminal.

Multiplexing can create a more economical use of the communication channels. When the input from several terminals is combined into a single input stream, data from these terminals can be sent over a single channel. At the receiving end, a similar unit separates the previously combined input streams for processing.

A concentrator differs from a multiplexer in that it allows data from only one terminal at a time to be transmitted over a communication channel. The concentrator polls the terminals one at a time to see if they have any messages to send. When a communication channel is free, the first terminal ready to send or receive data will get control of the channel and will continue to control it for the length of the transmission. The use of a concentrator relies on the assumption that not all terminals will be ready to send or receive data at a single given time. Figure 2–30 shows examples of communication systems using multiplexers and concentrators.

FIGURE 2–30 Communication Systems with Multiplexers and Concentrators

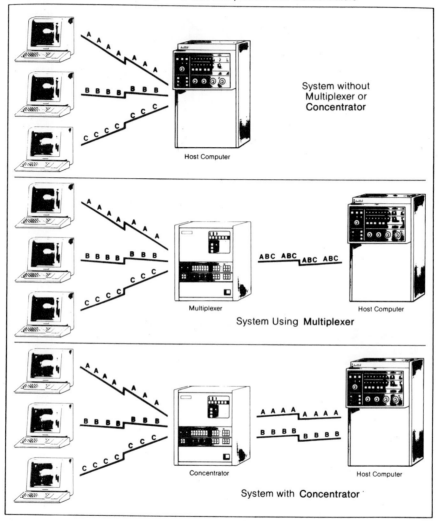

Programmable Communications Processors A **programmable communications processor** is a device that relieves the CPU of many of the tasks typically required in a communication system. When the volume of data transmission surpasses a certain level, a programmable communications processor can handle certain tasks more economically than the CPU. Examples of such tasks include handling messages and priorities, disconnecting after messages have been received, and verifying successfully transmitted messages.

The two most frequent uses of communications processors are message-switching and front-end processing. The principal task of the processor used for **message-switching** is to receive messages and route them to appropriate destinations. A **front-end processor** performs message-switching as well as more sophisticated operations such as validating transmitted data and preprocessing data before it is transmitted to the central computer.

COMPUTER SIZES AND CONFIGURATIONS
Mainframes

At the heart of a large-scale computer system is the **mainframe,** or CPU (which consists, as you recall, of control unit, ALU, and primary storage). A mainframe can process large amounts of data at very high speeds, hold up to millions of characters in its primary storage, and support many input, output, and auxiliary storage devices.

The mainframe sector is the backbone of the computer industry. Major competitors in this market are International Business Machines (IBM), Burroughs, Honeywell, Univac, National Cash Register (NCR), Control Data Corporation (CDC), and Amdahl. These vendors appeal to potential users of large, sophisticated computers.

Entry into the market is restricted by the huge capital investment required. However, once in the market, companies can spread the costs of research and development, application and system software, and hardware design over a number of units; this gives them a pricing advantage.

An example of a mainframe computer is any member of IBM's System/370 series. This series includes many models, and an organization can choose the model best suited to its processing needs. Other vendors in the mainframe sector also offer computers in various sizes with various processing speeds and storage capabilities. Purchase costs of these computers range from $200,000 to $1 million or more.

Though the mainframe sector dominates the computer industry, it has lost part of its market share during the past decade because of the changing nature of the computer business. The price of a computer system was dominated by the cost of the hardware; software costs were included in the total system price (in a selling technique called **bundling**). With recent technological advances, the cost of hardware has been declining at a rate of 15 to 20 percent per year. In contrast, software and service costs have increased significantly.

Another change in the computer industry is the trend toward distributed processing and away from centralized processing. The demand for larger, central-site computer systems has been replaced by a demand for smaller, more flexible systems. Mainframe vendors who have specialized in the production of large CPUs are diversifying into other sectors of the computer industry to remain competitive.

Many companies requiring the processing capabilities of large computers have already had them for some time. Purchases of newer processors are made only when the company needs expanded capacity or when new price/performance ratios make them cost-effective. The costs of maintaining large computer systems deter many firms from acquiring them. Some users are finding it more economical to purchase small computer systems. Since few users require the power of a supercomputer, the potential market for those large computers is limited. The needs of the high-end user are being met, but demands for sophistication and performance continue to challenge the creativity and abilities of manufacturers.

Supercomputers

Mainframe vendors sell their products to organizations that require extensive data-processing capabilities. These organizations may process vast amounts of data or may need to perform millions of calculations per second. In some cases, demand exists for even higher processing speeds and efficiency. To respond to these needs, some vendors offer very large, sophisticated computers called **supercomputers.**

Supercomputer systems are very expensive. The CRAY computers, developed by Cray Research, Incorporated, are examples of supercomputer systems. The CRAY–1 was offered at a base price of $4.5 million. These computers are used mainly in the scientific areas of weather forecasting, nuclear-weapons development, and energy supply and conservation. Other supercomputers are used by large corporations and government agencies where the needs for large data bases and complex calculation capabilities justify the costs of obtaining them.

Minicomputers

Minicomputers have come a long way since their initial development for specific applications such as process control and engineering calculations.

Current minicomputers are more flexible, provide greater capabilities, and support a full line of **peripherals,** such as input/output devices, auxiliary storage devices, and so on (Figure 2–31). The growth in minicomputer applications has led to the concept of distributed processing. Minicomputers are also used in timesharing applications, numerical control of machine tools, industrial automation, and word processing.

The distinction between minicomputers and mainframes has blurred over the past decade. The minicomputers manufactured today are more powerful than the mainframes manufactured ten years ago. Their prices range from $15,000 to about $250,000.

One reason for the popularity of the minicomputer is its flexibility. Minicomputers can be plugged into standard electrical outlets, they

FIGURE 2–31 A Minicomputer System

often do not require special facilities such as air conditioning and water cooling, and they can be used in an unlimited number of configurations. For example, a minicomputer system for a small firm may consist of a visual-display terminal, disk-storage unit, and a printer. A large distributed system may consist of hundreds of minicomputers and peripherals tied together by communication channels to meet the needs of a geographically dispersed organization.

The minicomputer industry has been growing at a rate of 35 to 40 percent annually. However, recent analysis indicates that the growth rate of this sector of the market is declining and may stabilize in the near future. Leading manufacturers include Digital Equipment Corporation (DEC), Hewlett-Packard, Data General, Honeywell, General Automation, and Texas Instruments.

Distributed Processing In many cases, minicomputers are used in conjunction with communication facilities to provide remote-processing capabilities. Most vendors in the minicomputer sector include data-communication equipment to provide powerful, flexible computing capabilities.

Prior to the advent of distributed processing, many organizations depended on large, centrally located computers. As user needs increased, these computers became overloaded. Centralized computer departments were not able to respond quickly to user requirements. Users began to replace or supplement their large computers with a number of minicomputers located where processing was required, reducing the workloads on the large computers. Figure 2–32 shows a distributed minicomputer system.

FIGURE 2–32 Distributed Minicomputer System

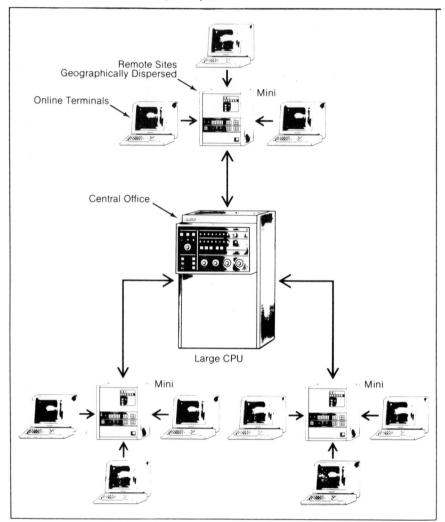

Remote Sites
Geographically Dispersed

Online Terminals

Mini

Central Office

Large CPU

Mini

Mini

Microcomputers

The microcomputer, or personal-computer, market has received a great deal of attention recently. When microcomputers first appeared, they were used by hobby-oriented engineers, programmers, electronics buffs, and other technically competent and inquisitive individuals. These people built their computers from scratch or purchased ready-to-assemble kits. The hobbyist could put together a real computer, complete with a keyboard for data entry and a TV-like display tube.

At the heart of a microcomputer is a microprocessor that performs arithmetic/logic operations and control functions, much as the CPU of a large computer does. The microprocessor fits on a single silicon chip the size of a nail head (Figure 2–33). Some cost under $10. Memory and input/output units are then added, as on a large mainframe computer, making microcomputers very powerful for their size.

At the sight of a true consumer market, manufacturers began to offer user-oriented microcomputer systems. These small systems were preassembled and equipped with programs to do simple jobs, such as balancing a checkbook or playing a game of backgammon. The personal-computer market started in 1975 with the introduction of the Altair 8800, a computer kit for less than $500. Today a wide range of personal computers offers complete computing capabilities at low costs. A computer for the home can be purchased for about the same price as a good stereo system; those available range in price from $100 to $5,000.

Prior to 1982, the most popular personal computer systems were the Apple, TRS-80, and PET Commodore. Then IBM entered the market and proved an immediate success with a personal computer priced to compete with the top of the line home computers. This experience led IBM to enter the smaller home computer market with the IBM Personal Junior in 1984. Other large computer manufacturers, such as Digital Equipment Corporation, and toy manufacturers, such as Coleco, offer their own microcomputers. However, at the same time, a shakeup occurred in the industry with such companies as Texas Instruments departing and Atari suffering catastrophic losses.

Applications Profitable applications of microcomputers are found in small businesses and in the professions. An estimated one-third of all personal computers are located in private offices, where businesspeople can use them to do word processing, accounting, inventory control,

FIGURE 2–33 Microprocessor on a Chip

order processing, customer lists, client records, tax records, mailing labels, and evaluation of bids and contracts. School teachers can use them to devise exams and compute grades; doctors, to keep patients' records; and college football coaches, to figure out potent combinations of players and strategies.

The use of personal computers in small businesses has led to a new phenomenon known as telecommuting. **Telecommuting** is based on computer hookups between offices and homes that allow employees to work at home. This concept enables firms to employ labor resources that might not otherwise be available. For example, handicapped people, women who leave jobs to raise families but still want to work, and commuters who find the cost of gasoline prohibitive can be gainfully employed. Work can be done at all hours of the day.

Another area influenced by the low cost of microcomputers is **word processing,** the manipulation of text data to achieve a desired output. Wang Laboratories is the leading manufacturer of word-processing equipment, but many other manufacturers are also developing word processors.

A typical stand-alone word-processing system consists of a keyboard, a visual-display screen, a storage unit, and a printer (Figure 2–34). An operator enters text (in the form of memos, letters, reports, and the like) on the keyboard. The text is stored and can be edited, revised, and reformatted without retyping entire documents. The printer is used to generate hard copies when desired. Another advantage is the word processor's ability to store names and addresses that can be used in form letters or for distribution of output.

Computer Stores   Personal computing was, until recently, primarily a mail-order business. Products were shipped directly from manufacturers to users. With the emergence of the home-computer concept, however, a new retailing phenomenon has evolved—the computer store. These stores are structured to appeal to owners of small businesses and to personal users. Today, thousands of home-computer stores exist in the United States. The best ones offer a variety of products and services manufactured by several firms. Demonstration systems are on display so that potential buyers can experiment with the systems, much as they would take test drives before purchasing a car. Microcomputer experts are available to answer questions and to provide technical guidance to the computer novice.

Networks

A typical computer system consists of a single mainframe linked to a variety of peripherals. If the peripherals are connected directly to the CPU, the system is said to be a **local system.** However, when communication channels are used, terminals may be far removed from the

FIGURE 2–34 Display Word-Processing System with a Daisy Wheel Printer

mainframe. These terminals, connected to the central computer by a communication channel, make up a **remote system.** When several CPUs are linked together by communication channels, they form a **network** or a **distributed data processing system.** Together, these computers allow faster response to inquiries and provide the power needed to perform complex calculations.

As with a single CPU and its terminals, the network's mainframes may be hooked together to form either local or remote systems. Several computers can be connected at a central location to enhance computing capabilities. Or, the same computers can be dispersed geographically to the location of data collection or information retrieval, forming a distributed system.

Different types of structures can be used to implement the multiple CPU concept (Figure 2–35). In a **star configuration,** all transactions must go through a central computer before being routed to the appropriate network computer. The effect is to create a central decision point. This facilitates workload distribution and resource sharing, but it exposes the system to single-point vulnerability. An alternative approach uses a number of computers connected to a single transmission line in a **ring configuration.** This type of system can bypass a malfunctioning unit without disrupting operations throughout the network.

FIGURE 2–35 Multiple CPU Configurations

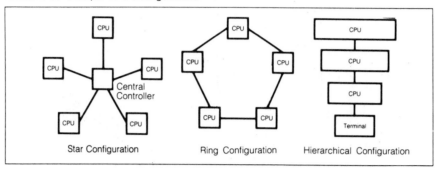

Star Configuration   Ring Configuration   Hierarchical Configuration

An interesting and more sophisticated approach is the **hierarchical network.** With this approach, an organization's needs are divided into multiple levels that receive different levels of computer support. The lowest is the user level, where only routine-transaction computing power is supplied, but this level is connected to the next higher level and its associated information system. At each higher level, the machine size increases while the need for distribution decreases. Thus, such a system consists of a network of small computers tied into a large central computing complex.

Figure 2–36 shows a distributed system consisting of three dispersed minicomputers connected by communication linkages to a large central computer. The three minicomputers are located in three functional departments of the organization—finance, marketing, and production. Thus, the functional departments can meet their processing requirements locally. Some of the information generated by the minicomputers is communicated to the central computer to be used in corporate-wide planning and control. Such a network provides fast response and great flexibility to local system users. Furthermore, the central facility is available to them for jobs that require computing power beyond the capabilities of the minicomputers.

It is easy to see how the use of networks can greatly enhance a business's data-processing facilities. As more office functions become automated (like word processing) and more applications for minicomputers and microcomputers are developed, computer networks will undoubtedly become one of the more important parts of the data-processing environment.

SUMMARY

• Instructions are placed in consecutive locations in the computer's memory so that they can be accessed and executed consecutively. This process is called the next-sequential-instruction feature.

FIGURE 2–36 Distributed System

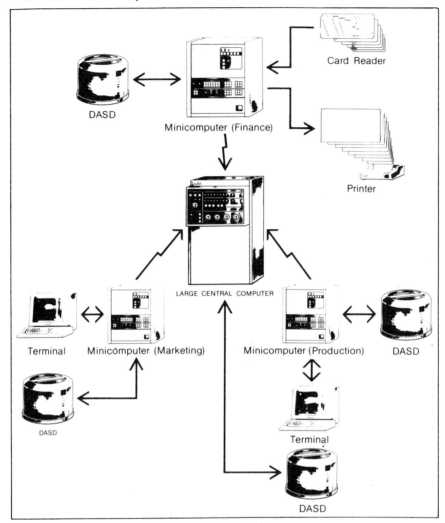

● The stored-program concept involves storing both data and instructions in the computer's memory. This allows the computer to process at its own speed.

● Nondestructive read/destructive write allows data and instructions to be reread as many times as required for processing until new data or instructions are placed over them.

● The central processing unit, the heart of the computer, is composed of three units: the primary-storage unit, the arithmetic/logic unit (ALU), and the control unit. The control unit maintains order and controls what is happening in the CPU; the ALU handles the execution of all arithmetic and logic operations; and the primary-storage unit is the internal section that holds all data and instructions necessary for processing.

● Data representation in the computer is based on a two-state or binary system. A 1 in a position indicates the presence of a power of two, whereas a 0 indicates its absence. The binary-coded decimal (BCD) system uses only four binary digits to represent any decimal integer; the Extended Binary-Coded Decimal Interchange Code (EBCDIC) system permits the representation of numeric, alphabetic, and special characters with an eight-digit coding system. The American Standard Code for Information Interchange (ASCII) is a 7- or 8-bit coding system often used in small computer systems.

● The most common type of primary storage today is semiconductor storage. Semiconductor storage is compact and fast, but is volatile; it requires a constant power source to maintain the stored data. Older computers used magnetic-core storage, wherein binary digits (bits) were represented using tiny, magnetized iron-alloy rings. Bubble-memory technology uses charged "bubbles" on a magnetic film to represent data. Bubble memory is faster and smaller than core memory. Bubble memory, like core memory, is nonvolatile.

● Read-only memory (ROM) is the part of the hardware of the computer where programming instructions are stored in unalterable form. New versions of ROM include programmable read-only memory (PROM) and erasable programmable read-only memory (EPROM).

● The punched card is capable of holding eighty characters of data in the form of numbers, letters, and special characters through the presence or absence of punched holes in the card columns.

● Key-to-tape and key-to-disk systems use a magnetic medium to store data. Unlike cards, new data can be stored over old data that is no longer required.

● Magnetic tape is similar to tape-recorder tape in that data can be recorded, played back at a later time, or erased (and the tape used to carry other data). Magnetic tape stores data as magnetized bits, with individual records separated by a series of interrecord gaps.

● A magnetic-disk unit is a direct-access storage device. Data is found by accessing the surface number, the track number, and the position of the data on the track.

● Source-data automation refers to capturing data about an event when and where it occurs. Examples include magnetic-ink character readers; optical-recognition (optical mark and optical character) devices, and remote input using point-of-sale (POS) terminals, touch-tone devices, and voice-recognition systems. Intelligent terminals can perform data verification and edits before submitting input to the main computer.

● There are impact and nonimpact printers. Impact printers are either line-at-a-time or character-at-a-time printers. Nonimpact printers use electrostatic, electrothermal, ink-jet, laser, and xerographic methods.

● Special-purpose output is designed to provide information in a particular way or format. Visual-display terminals (also called CRTs) provide soft-copy output of computer information. Plotters provide information summarized and interpreted into graphic form. Computer-output microfilm (COM) stores data in reduced size on photographic film.

● A channel is a small, limited-capacity computer that handles slow-speed input/output operations, thus relieving the CPU of its responsibility for data transfer.

● The mainframe sector of the computer industry is limited to a few large companies. This sector dominates the computer industry; however, entry into this market is limited by the huge capital investment needed. Mainframe vendors provide software support and maintenance in various ways. These costs may or may not be included in the initial purchase or lease price.

● Supercomputer systems are capable of processing large amounts of data and performing millions of calculations per second. These systems are very expensive and are used by large corporations and government agencies that need to support large data bases and complex calculations.

● The declining costs of hardware along with the trends toward distributed processing have resulted in a changing computer industry. Mainframe vendors have found it profitable to diversify into other market areas.

● Minicomputer systems have led to the concept of distributed processing. Minicomputers are flexible and can support many peripherals. When combined with data-communication equipment, they can be very powerful data-processing tools. Vendors in this market include software and services in their product offerings. In addition, software companies supply various types of software packages. Organizations can purchase prewritten packages or develop programs in-house.

● Microcomputers have rapidly gained popularity in homes, small businesses, and large corporations. Personal computers offer homeowners and hobbyists a wide variety of electronic games, and also perform household duties. Small businesses and professions use microcomputers to perform clerical tasks such as payroll, accounts receivable, appointment scheduling, and billing. Telecommuting allows employees to work at home on computer terminals tied to offices. Large corporations use computers to provide desktop conveniences for managers.

● Word-processing systems ease the typing duties of secretaries in all sizes of organizations. Word processing can be provided by a stand-alone microcomputer, by a distributed minicomputer system, or by a large system.

● A multitude of software and peripheral devices can be used with microcomputers. The microcomputer sector has evolved to serve a mass-merchandise, retail market. Both hardware and software are available at local computer stores. Prospective microcomputer users must consider the importance of software support when buying computer systems.

REVIEW QUESTIONS

1. Read-only memory
   a. can be changed by regular program instructions.
   b. is the same as nondestructive-read internal storage.
   c. can be written over.
   d. can be rewired to change instructions.

2. Any of the decimal integers (0 through 9) can be represented in the binary-coded decimal (BCD) system with _____ binary digits.
   a. two
   b. four
   c. ten
   d. twelve

3. Compared with large computers, minicomputers generally have
   a. no means of being connected to a printer.
   b. a control unit and primary storage, but no ALU.
   c. a control unit and ALU, but no primary-storage unit.
   d. smaller memories.

4. Which of the following is not a function of the CPU control unit?
   a. Directs sequence of operations
   b. Interprets instructions
   c. Processes and stores data
   d. Initiates commands

5. In the binary-coded decimal (BCD) system, which of the following code patterns represents 629?
   a. 0110–0010–1001
   b. 1001110101
   c. 1001–1101–1001
   d. 0010–0111–1010

6. A channel is a(an)
   a. input/output device.
   b. radio wavelength.
   c. small, limited-capacity computer.
   d. wire connecting the CPU and input/output devices.

7. Tape records
   a. are restricted to a certain record length.
   b. are restricted to definite character size.
   c. are rarely read in their entirety, all at once.
   d. can be no longer than the field size specified for the file.

8. The binary number 1010111 is equivalent to the decimal number
   a. 185.
   b. 75.
   c. 71.
   d. 87.

9. The decimal number 68 is equivalent in value to the binary number
   a. 1000100.
   b. 101000.
   c. 100010.
   d. 110010.

10. The access mechanism allows
    a. the CPU to access primary storage.
    b. the printer to use its paper supply.
    c. the read/write head to be positioned over the appropriate disk track.
    d. the computer operator to enter the interior of the machine.

11. Secondary storage devices are
    a. very expensive to maintain as compared with core devices.
    b. comprised of tiny iron "doughnuts."
    c. used only for special purposes.
    d. similar to main memory.

12. Minicomputers are
    a. used to replace manual data-processing methods.
    b. used by large firms to form minicomputer networks.
    c. applicable to only a few tasks.
    d. both (a) and (b).

13. Wand readers are used for
    a. reading magnetic tape.
    b. reading Universal Product Codes.
    c. audio response.
    d. card readers.

14. A multiplexer channel can read data from more than one device at a time. It is used with input/output devices such as
    a. printers and terminals.
    b. magnetic-tape and disk units.
    c. card readers and magnetic-tape units.
    d. magnetic-disk units, printers, and card readers.

15. Which of the following is not a slow-speed input/output device?
    a. Punched-card reader
    b. Magnetic-tape unit
    c. Printer
    d. Both (a) and (c) are not slow-speed devices.

16. The smallest amount of data a computer can store is known as a
    a. bit.
    b. byte.
    c. core.
    d. sentence.

17. A 32 K storage unit can store approximately how many characters coded in EBCDIC?
    a. 32
    b. 32,000
    c. 64,000
    d. 256,000

18. Which of the following codes is in odd parity?
    a. 0–1111–0011
    b. 1–1111–0001
    c. 0–1111–1111
    d. 1–1111–1001

19. Which of the following memory devices is volatile?
    a. Core storage
    b. Semiconductor storage
    c. Bubble memory
    d. All of the above are nonvolatile.

20. The fastest printers are
    a. ink-jet printers.
    b. electrostatic printers.
    c. electrothermal printers.
    d. laser printers.

SOFTWARE TECHNOLOGY

When a problem is to be solved with the assistance of a computer, certain procedures must be followed to prepare the problem so that the computer can be used. Despite the apparent complexity and power of the computer, it is merely a tool that must be manipulated by an individual. Step-by-step instructions that provide the problem solution are required. This series of instructions is known as a program, and the individual who creates the program is known as a programmer.

LEVELS OF PROGRAMS

There are two basic types of programs: (1) **applications programs** that solve user problems (such as payroll), and (2) **system programs** that coordinate the operation of all computer circuitry. The term *software* is used to describe both types of computer programs; the term *hardware* is used to describe the electrical circuitry and physical devices that make up the computer system, which we examined in Part Two. (The term **firmware** is often applied to programs built into the computer, such as the mathematical functions found in read-only memory.)

System programming usually is provided by the computer manufacturer or by a specialized programming firm. System programs directly affect the running of the computer. They are designed to facilitate the use of the hardware and to help the computer system run quickly and efficiently. System programs are initially written in a general fashion to meet all possible requirements that a computer facility may have to handle; they can be modified by in-house programmers to meet an organization's specific needs.

System programmers keep the system programs in good running order and tailor them to meet organization requirements when necessary. Since system programmers serve as a bridge between the computer and **applications programmers,** they must have the technical background required to understand the complex internal operations of a computer. Because each organization has a different assortment of applications programs to be run, system programs must be modified (tuned) to ensure computer efficiency at each organization's installation.

Applications programs, on the other hand, solve problems facing organization management. They are generally developed within an organization, although some can be purchased. The job of the applications programmer is to use the capabilities of the computer in solving a specific problem. Typical examples of applications programs are those for inventory control and accounting. Applications programmers working for banks write programs to update customer accounts. Because of the work of the system programmer, the work of the applications programmer can be done without an in-depth knowledge of the computer.

Operating Systems

In early computer systems, human operators monitored computer operations, determined the order in which submitted programs were run (the priority), and readied input and output devices. While early electronic development increased the processing speeds of CPUs, the speed of human operators remained constant. Time delays and errors caused by human-operator intervention became a serious problem.

In the 1960s, operating systems were developed to help overcome this problem. An **operating system** is a collection of programs used by the computer to manage its own operations. This approach provides a control system that can operate at computer speeds. Instead of a human operator, the operating system is given the responsibility for all jobs to be run.

Types of Operating Systems   There are two basic types of operating systems: **batch (stacked) job** and real time. In a stacked-job processing environment, several user programs (jobs or job steps) are grouped into a batch and processed one after the other in a continuous stream. A real-time operating system can respond to spontaneous requests for system resources, such as management inquiries entered from terminals.

Many operating systems can handle both batch and real-time applications simultaneously. These systems direct processing of a job stream but also respond to interrupts from other devices, such as terminals, in direct communication with the CPU. (An **interrupt** is a condition or event that temporarily suspends normal processing operations—for example, a request to accept data from an input device or a request for transfer of data to an output device.)

Components   An operating system is an integrated collection of subsystems. Each subsystem consists of programs that perform specific duties (Figure 3–1). Since all operating-system programs work as a

FIGURE 3–1 Operating System in Primary Storage and System Residence Device

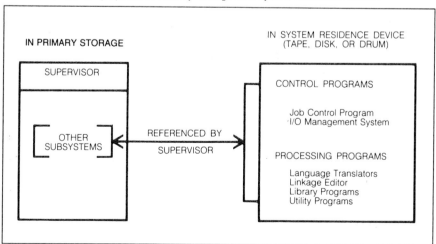

team, CPU idle time is avoided and use of computer facilities is increased. Operating-system programs are usually stored on an auxiliary device known as the **system-residence device.** They are called into primary storage when needed.

Although operating systems allow the computer to direct its own operations, they do have some disadvantages. Space must be provided in primary storage for operating programs. This is space that otherwise could be used by applications programs. Since this space must be reserved, it is called **overhead.** The computer must constantly refer back to operating-system programs in order to know what to do next. In doing so, some 50 percent of processing time is taken up by operating-system programs.

Two types of programs make up the operating system: control programs and processing programs. **Control programs** oversee system operations and perform tasks such as input/output, scheduling, handling interrupts, and communicating with the computer operator or programmers. **Processing programs** are executed under the supervision of control programs and are used by the programmer to simplify program preparation for the computer system.

Control Programs. The **supervisor program** (also called the **monitor** or **executive**), the major component of the operating system, coordinates the activities of all other parts of the operating system. When the computer is first put into use, the supervisor is the first program to be transferred into primary storage from the system-residence device. The supervisor schedules input/output operations and allocates resources to various input/output devices. It also sends messages to the computer operator, indicating the status of particular jobs, error conditions, and so on.

The operating system requires job-control information in order to perform its mission. (A **job** is a unit of work to be processed by the CPU.) A **job-control language (JCL)** serves as the communication link between the programmer and the operating system. Job-control statements are used to identify the beginning of a job, to identify the specific program to be executed, to describe the work to be done, and to indicate the input/output devices required. The **job-control program** translates the job-control statements (written by a programmer) into machine-language instructions that can be executed by the computer.

The control programs of the operating system must be able to control and coordinate the CPU while receiving input, executing instruction of programs in storage, and regulating output. Input/output devices must be assigned to specific programs, and data must be moved between them and specific memory locations. The **input/output management system** oversees and coordinates these processes.

Processing Programs. The operating system contains several processing programs that facilitate efficient processing operations by simplifying program preparation and execution for users. The major processing programs contained in the operating system are the language translators, linkage editor, library programs, and utility programs.

A **language-translator program,** also known as a **compiler,** translates English-like programs (such as FORTRAN or COBOL) written by programmers into machine-language instructions. The original, untranslated program is called the **source program.** The translated application program is called the **object program,** and often remains on the system-residence device until the supervisor calls for it to be loaded into primary storage for execution. It is the task of the **linkage editor** to "link" the object program from the system-residence device to main storage by assigning appropriate main-storage addresses to each byte of the object program.

Some interactive languages on small computer systems use an interpreter rather than a compiler to translate source statements to object code. Unlike a compiler, which translates an entire program at one time (for later execution), an **interpreter** evaluates and translates program statements as the program is executed, one instruction at a time. The interpreter takes one source-program instruction, translates it into machine code, and then executes it. It then takes the next instruction, translates it, and so on. Using an interpreter can save space, since the interpreter program itself can be quite small, and it eliminates the need to store the program's translated object code in the computer. It may also be inefficient—program statements that are used multiple times must be translated each time they are executed.

Library programs are user-written or manufacturer-supplied programs and subroutines that are frequently used on other programs. So these routines will not have to be rewritten every time they are needed, they are stored in a **system library** (usually on magnetic disk or tape) and called into main storage when needed. They are then linked together with other programs to perform specific tasks. A **librarian program** manages the storage and use of library programs by maintaining a directory of programs in the system library; it also contains appropriate procedures for adding and deleting programs.

Operating systems also include a set of **utility programs** that perform specialized functions. For example, a utility program can be used to transfer data from tape to tape, tape to disk, card to tape, or tape to printer. Other utility programs, known as **sort/merge programs,** are used to order (sort) records into a particular sequence to facilitate updating of files. Once sorted, several files can be merged to form a single, updated file. Job-control statements are used to specify the sort and merge programs; these programs or routines are then called into main storage when needed.

Languages

As computers have developed in complexity, so have programming languages. Today there are three sets of language groups, known as machine languages, assembly languages, and higher-level languages (Figure 3–2).

Levels   **Machine language** is as old as the computer itself. It is the code that designates the proper electrical states in the computer. Machine language is a combination of 0s and 1s and is the only language the computer can execute directly. It can therefore be called the language of the computer. Each type of computer has its own machine language. That language is not transferable to another type of computer. Each machine-language instruction must specify not only what operation is to be done, but also where the items to be operated on are stored. Because of these specification requirements, programming is extremely complex, tedious, and time-consuming. A machine-language program has no obvious meaning to people not skilled in deciphering the 0 and 1 combinations.

Because machine-language programming is difficult, other languages have been developed to save programming time and reduce complexity. **Assembly language** is close to machine language but one step removed in the direction of human understanding. Programmers who are using assembly languages must be very conscious of the computer and must designate not only operations to be performed but also data-storage locations. This requirement is similar to that of machine language. However, instead of the 0 and 1 groupings of machine language, convenient symbols and abbreviations are used in writing programs. For instance, "STO" may stand for STORE, and "TRA" for TRANSFER. Even with these conveniences, programming in assembly language is cumbersome, although not as difficult as machine-language programming.

Higher-level languages are the user friendly programming languages. They are procedure- and problem-oriented, designed so that most of the programmer's attention can be directed to how a problem is solved rather than to how the computer is operated. (Some of the newest programming languages are being referred to as very-high-level;

FIGURE 3–2 Language Levels

Degree of User Orientation		Degree of Machine Orientation
Low	Machine Language	High
↓	Assembly Language	↓
High	High-level Language	Low

these describe what problem is to be solved, rather than how it is to be solved.) Higher-level languages are the farthest removed from the hardware; they least resemble the 0 and 1 combinations of machine language. Whereas one assembly-language instruction is generally equivalent to one machine-language instruction, one higher-level-language statement can accomplish the same result as a half dozen or more machine-language instructions. One principal reason for this is that addresses for many of the required storage locations do not need to be specified; they are handled more easily by the use of symbolic names, or **variables,** such as TAX or GROSS-PAY. Many higher-level languages are algebraic or English-like and allow the use of common mathematical terms and symbols. The time and effort needed to write a program are reduced, and programs are easier to correct or modify. For comparison, look at the programs in Figures 3–3 and 3–4. Figure 3–4 is the higher-level-language equivalent of the program in Figure 3–3.

Popular Higher-Level Languages Machine-language and assembly-language programs are written for a particular model of computer and cannot generally be executed on another model. Programs in higher-level languages are usually **machine-independent,** which means that they can be transferred from one model to another with little change. Thousands of higher-level languages have been developed. Among them are FORTRAN, COBOL, PL/I, RPG, BASIC, Pascal, and APL. Each has its own advantages, disadvantages, and applications.

FORTRAN. **FORTRAN** (*FORmula TRANslator*) is the oldest higher-level programming language. It originated in the mid-1950s, when most programs were written in either assembly language or machine language. Efforts were made to develop a programming language that resembled English and algebra but could be translated into machine language by the computer. This effort, backed by IBM, produced FORTRAN—the first commercially available high-level language (Figure 3–5). When FORTRAN was developed, the computer was used primarily by engineers, scientists, and mathematicians. Consequently, FORTRAN was designed to meet their needs. FORTRAN is especially applicable where numerous complex arithmetic calculations are necessary, and it is also used in many business applications. However, it is not well suited for programs involving maintenance of files, editing of data, or production of documents.

COBOL. **COBOL** (*COmmon Business-Oriented Language*) is the most frequently used business programming language. Before 1960, no language well suited to solving business problems existed. Business applications generally involve large amounts of input and output. Unlike scientific applications, business applications do not usually require that the computer be capable of performing complex mathematical computations. With this in mind, the U.S. Department of Defense called

FIGURE 3–3 Payroll Program in Assembly Language

```
         SOURCE  STATEMENT
                 START
PAYROLL          BALR      12,0  ⎫
                 USING     *,12  ⎬  Set Up Registers
                 XPRNT     HEADING,45 }  Print Headings
READCRD          XREAD     CARD80      ⎫
                 CLC       EOF,''C'99'  ⎬  Read Data Card
                 BE        DONE        ⎭
                 PACK      WKHR!,HOURS  ⎫
                 PACK      WKRATE,RATE  ⎬  Convert Data to
                 ZAP       GROSS,ZERO      Decimal
                 ZAP       OVRTME,ZERO     Form and Initialize
                 ZAP       REG,ZERO        Variables
                 CP        WKHRS,FORTY  ⎫
                 BH        OVERTIME     ⎬
                 AP        GROSS,WKRATE    Compute Regular Pay
                 MP        GROSS,WKHRS
                 B         TAXRATE      ⎭
OVERTIME         AP        OVRTME, FORTY  ⎫
                 MP        OVRTME,WKRATE
                 AP        GROSS,WKRATE
                 SP        WKHRS,FORTY     Compute
                 MP        WKHRS,ONEHLF    Overtime
                 MP        GROSS,WKHRS     Pay
                 MVN       GROSS+5(1),GROSS+6
                 ZAP       GROSS(7),GROSS(6)
                 AP        GROSS,OVRTME  ⎭
TAXRATE          CP        GROSS,=P'25000'  ⎫
                 BH        UPPERRTE
                 ZAP       RATE,LOW         Determine
                 B         TAXES            Tax Rate
UPPERRTE         ZAP       RATE,HIGH     ⎭
TAXES            ZAP       TOTAXES,GROSS    ⎫
                 MP        TOTAXES,RATE
                 AP        TOTAXES,=P'50'   Compute
                 MVN       TOTAXES+5(1),TOTAXES+6  Taxes
                 ZAP       TOTAXES(7),TOTAXES(6)  ⎭
                 SP        GROSS,TOTAXES ⎫  Calculate Net Pay
                 MVC       PRPAY,MASK    ⎬  and Edit Print Line
                 ED        PRPAY,GROSS   ⎭
                 MVC       PRNAME,NAME   ⎫  Print Output Line
                 XPRNT     LINE,32       ⎭
         SOURCE  STATEMENT
                 B         READCRD
DONE             XPRNT     HEADING,1
                 BR        14
*
*
*
```

together representatives of computer users, manufacturers, and government installations to examine the feasibility of establishing a common programming language for businesses. That was the beginning of the CODASYL (Conference Of DAta SYstems Languages) committee. By 1960, the committee had established the specifications for COBOL, and

FIGURE 3-3 Continued

```
CARD       DS    0CL80   ⌉
NAME       DS    CL16    │
HOURS      DS    CL2     │   Input Card File
           DS    CL2     ├   Definitions
RATE       DS    CL4     │
           DS    CL54    │
EOF        DS    CL2     ⌋
HEADING    DS    0CL45   ⌉
           DC    CL1'1'  │
           DC    CL13,EMPLOYEE NAME' │
           DC    CL10'   │
           DC    CL7'NET PAY'  │   Output Print
           DC    CL14' '  ├   File Definitions
LINE       DS    0CL30   │
           DC    CL1' '  │
PRNAME     DS    CL16    │
PRPAY      DS    CL15    ⌋
GROSS      DS    PL7     ⌉
WKRATE     DS    PL3     │
OVRTME     DS    PL7     │
REG        DS    PL7     │
WKHRS      DS    PL4     │
FORTY      DC    PL2'40' ├   Variable Definitions
ONEHLF     DC    PL2'150'│
LOW        DC    PL2'14' │
HIGH       DC    PL2'20' │
ZERO       DC    PL4'0000' │
TOTAXES    DS    PL7     ⌋
MASK       DC    X'402020202020202020202021482121' ⌉   Edit Field
           END   PAYROLL
                 =C'99'
                 =P'50'
                 =P'25000'
```

Output:

```
EMPLOYEE NAME          NET PAY

LYNN MANGINO           224.00
THOMAS RITTER          212.42
MARIE OLSON            209.00
LORI DUNLEVY           172.00
WILLIAM WILSON         308.00
```

the first commercial versions of the language were offered later that year. The government furthered its cause in the mid–1960s by refusing to buy or lease any computer that could not process a program written in COBOL. COBOL programs consist of English-like sentences and paragraphs. Consequently, they can be interpreted even by nonprogrammers. This feature is also a disadvantage of COBOL, since programs are very wordy and can be tedious to write. Every COBOL program requires four divisions, with strict rules about contents (Figure 3–4). Nonetheless, COBOL is the dominant language in use today in both business and the federal government.

FIGURE 3–4 Payroll Program in COBOL

```
IDENTIFICATION DIVISION.
PROGRAM-ID. PAYROLL.
ENVIRONMENT DIVISION.
INPUT-OUTPUT SECTION.
FILE-CONTROL.
    SELECT CARD-FILE ASSIGN TO UR-2540R-S-SYSIN.
    SELECT PRINT-FILE ASSIGN TO UR-S-SYSPRINT.
DATA DIVISION.
FILE SECTION.
FD  CARD-FILE LABEL RECORDS ARE OMITTED.
01  PAY-CARD.
    02 EMPLOYEE-NAME PICTURE A(16).
    02 HOURS-WORKED PICTURE 99.
    02 WAGE-PER-HOUR PICTURE 99V99.
FD  PRINT-FILE LABEL RECORDS ARE OMITTED.
01  PRINT-LINE.
    02 NAME        PICTURE A(16).
    02 FILLER      PICTURE X(5).
    02 AMOUNT      PICTURE ****.99.
WORKING-STORAGE SECTION.
77  GROSS-PAY      PICTURE 999V99.
77  REGULAR-PAY    PICTURE 999V99.
77  OVERTIME-PAY   PICTURE 999V99.
77  NET-PAY        PICTURE 999V99.
77  TAX            PICTURE 999V99.
77  OVERTIME-HOURS PICTURE 99.
77  OVERTIME-RATE  PICTURE 999V999.
77  BLANK-LINE     PICTURE X(132) VALUE SPACES.
PROCEDURE DIVISION.
    DISPLAY 'EMPLOYEE NAME          ', 'NET PAY'.
    DISPLAY BLANK-LINE.
    OPEN INPUT CARD-FILE, OUTPUT PRINT-FILE.
```

PL/I. **PL/I** *(Programming Language One)* was designed as an all-purpose language that would combine the best features of FORTRAN and COBOL (Figure 3–6). Thus, PL/I was the first higher-level language intended for use in both scientific and business applications. Furthermore, it was designed to be compatible with the philosophy of structured programming, a technique in which long programs are written in a building-block fashion, using a sequence of small program sections or modules. PL/I was developed by IBM in the early 1960s. The introduction of this language coincided with the introduction of IBM's System/360 computer, although other manufacturers support PL/I today. A subset of PL/I, called PL/C, was developed by Cornell University. PL/C is designed to aid beginning programmers in learning the language.

RPG. **RPG** *(Report Program Generator)* is a problem-oriented language originally designed to produce business reports. Basically, the programmer using RPG describes the type of report desired without having to specify much of the logic involved. A generator program is then used to build (generate) a program to produce the report. Therefore, little programming skill is required to use RPG. Since RPG was initially

FIGURE 3–4 Continued

```
WORK-LOOP.
    READ CARD-FILE AT END GO TO FINISH.
    IF HOURS-WORKED IS GREATER THAN 40 THEN GO TO
        OVERTIME-ROUTINE.
    MULTIPLY HOURS-WORKED BY WAGE-PER-HOUR GIVING GROSS-PAY.
    GO TO TAX-COMPUTATION.
OVERTIME-ROUTINE.
    MULTIPLY WAGE-PER-HOUR BY 40 GIVING REGULAR-PAY.
    SUBTRACT 40 FROM HOURS-WORKED GIVING OVERTIME-HOURS.
    MULTIPLY WAGE-PER-HOUR BY 1.5 GIVING OVERTIME-RATE.
    MULTIPLY OVERTIME-HOURS BY OVERTIME-RATE GIVING
        OVERTIME-PAY.
    ADD REGULAR-PAY, OVERTIME-PAY GIVING GROSS-PAY.
TAX-COMPUTATION.
    IF GROSS-PAY IS GREATER THAN 250 THEN MULTIPLY GROSS-PAY
        BY 0.20 GIVING TAX ELSE MULTIPLY GROSS-PAY BY 0.14
        GIVING TAX.
    SUBTRACT TAX FROM GROSS-PAY GIVING NET-PAY.
    MOVE EMPLOYEE-NAME TO NAME.
    MOVE NET-PAY TO AMOUNT.
    WRITE PRINT-LINE.
    GO TO WORK-LOOP.
FINISH.
    CLOSE CARD-FILE, PRINT-FILE.
    STOP RUN.
```

Output:

```
EMPLOYEE NAME           NET PAY

LYNN MANGINO            $224.00
THOMAS RITTER          $212.42
MARIE OLSON            $209.00
LORI DUNLEVY          $172.00
WILLIAM WILSON        $308.00
```

intended to support the logic of punched-card equipment, it is used primarily with small computer systems. Many firms that formerly used electromechanical punched-card processing equipment have upgraded their data-processing operations to small computer systems. These firms usually have relatively simple, straightforward data-processing needs. In such cases, a small computer system supporting RPG can provide significantly improved data-processing operations. Management reports can be produced in a fraction of the time required by electromechanical methods. RPG is easy to learn and use. Since it does not require large amounts of main storage, it is one of the primary languages of small computers and minicomputers. However, the computational capabilities of RPG are limited. Also, RPG is not a standardized language; therefore, RPG programs may require a significant degree of modification in order to be executed on another model of computer.

BASIC.   **BASIC** (*Beginner's All-purpose Symbolic Instruction Code*) was developed at Dartmouth College in the 1960s for use with timesharing

FIGURE 3-5 Payroll Program in FORTRAN

```
FORTRAN IV G LEVEL 21        MAIN              DATE = 84214

      WRITE (6,1)
1     FORMAT('1','EMPLOYEENAME',5X,'NETPAY'/'')
2     READ (5,3) NA,NB,NC,ND,NHOURS, WAGE, IEND
3     FORMAT (4A4, 12, 2X, F4.2, 54X, 12)
      IF (IEND. EQ.99) STOP
      IF (NHOURS.GT.40) GO TO 10
      GROSS = FLOAT(NHOURS)*WAGE
      GO TO 15
10    REG = 40.*WAGE
      OVERTM=FLOAT(NHOURS-40)*(1.5*WAGE)
      GROSS=REG+OVERTM
15    IF (GROSS.GT.250.) GO TO 20
      RATE = .14
      GO TO 25
20    RATE = .20
25    TAX=RATE*GROSS
      PAY = GROSS - TAX
      WRITE (6,50) NA,NB,NC,ND,PAY
50     FORMAT (' ', 4A4, 3X, F6.2)
      GO TO 2
      END

Output:

EMPLOYEE NAME     NET PAY

LYNN MANGINO      224.00
THOMAS RITTER     212.42
MARIE OLSON       209.00
LORI DUNLEVY      172.00
WILLIAM WILSON    308.00
```

systems. Because BASIC is easy to learn, it can be used by people with little or no programming experience—novice programmers can write fairly complex programs in BASIC in only a matter of hours (Figure 3–7). The growth in the use of timesharing systems has been accompanied by an increase in the use of BASIC. Most computer manufacturers offer BASIC support on their computers. Although BASIC was originally intended to be used by colleges and universities for instructional purposes, many companies have adopted it for their data-processing needs. In addition, the increasing popularity of microcomputers in homes is furthering the use of BASIC, since it is the language most often supported by these microcomputers. Among BASIC's most attractive features are its simplicity and flexibility. It is very easy to learn. It can be used for

FIGURE 3-6 Payroll Program in PL/I

```
PAYROLL: PROCEDURE OPTIONS (MAIN);

PAYROLL: PROCEDURE OPTIONS (MAIN);
DECLARE NAME       CHARACTER (16);
DECLARE HOURS      FIXED DECIMAL (2);
DECLARE WAGE       FIXED DECIMAL (3,2);
DECLARE GROSS_PAY FIXED DECIMAL(5,2);
DECLARE TAXRATE    FIXED DECIMAL (2,2);
DECLARE TAX        FIXED DECIMAL (4,2);
DECLARE NET_PAY    FIXED DECIMAL (5,2);
PUT PAGE LIST ('EMPLOYEE NAME', 'NET PAY');
PUT SKIP;
START: GET LIST (NAME, HOURS, WAGE);
ON ENDFILE GO TO FINISH;
IF HOURS>40 THEN
   GROSS_PAY→40*WAGE + 1.5*WAGE*(HOURS-40);
  ELSE GROSS_PAY=HOURS*WAGE;
IF GROSS_PAY>250 THEN TAXRATE=.20;
   ELSE TAXRATE=.14;
TAX=TAXRATE*GROSS_PAY;
NET_PAY=GROSS_PAY - TAX;
PUT SKIP (1) LIST (NAME, NET_PAY);
GO TO START;
FINISH: END PAYROLL

PAYROLL        14:50     AUGUST 3RD, 1981
```

Output:

```
EMPLOYEE NAME    NET PAY

LYNN MANGINO     224.00
THOMAS RITTER    212.42
MARIE OLSON      209.00
LORI DUNLEVY     172.00
WILLIAM WILSON   308.00
```

both scientific and business applications. And although BASIC was intended for use as an interactive programming language, it is finding increased use as a batch language.

PASCAL. **Pascal** is named after the French philosopher and mathematician, Blaise Pascal. (Remember from Part One that Pascal invented the first mechanical adding machine.) Niklaus Wirth, a computer scientist from Switzerland, developed Pascal between 1968 and 1970. The first Pascal compiler became available in 1971.

FIGURE 3-7 Payroll Program in BASIC

```
PAYROLL          14:50     AUGUST 3RD, 1984

10    REM THIS PROGRAM CALCULATES A WEEKLY
15    REM PAYROLL FOR FIVE EMPLOYEES
20    PRINT 'EMPLOYEE NAME', 'NET PAY'.
30    PRINT
40    READ N$, H, W
50    IF H > 40 THEN 70
60    LET G = H*W
65    GO TO 100
70    LET R = 40*W
80    LET O = (H-40) * (1.5*W)
90    LET G = R+O
100   IF G > 250 THEN 130
110   LET T = .14
120   GO TO 140
130   LET T = .20
140   LET T2 = T*G
150   LET P = G-T2
160   PRINT N$, P
170   GO TO 40
180   DATA 'LYNN MANGINO', 35, 8.00
190   DATA 'THOMAS RITTER', 48, 4.75
200   DATA 'MARIE OLSON', 45, 5.50
210   DATA 'LORI DUNLEVY', 40, 5.00
220   DATA 'WILLIAM WILSON', 50, 7.00
230   END

RUN PAYROLL

Output

PAYROLL

EMPLOYEE NAME     NET PAY

LYNN MANGINO      224.00
THOMAS RITTER     212.42
MARIE OLSON       209.00
LORI DUNLEVY      172.00
WILLIAM WILSON    308.00

LINE   40:   END  OF  DATA
```

Like BASIC, Pascal was first developed to teach programming concepts to students, but it is rapidly expanding beyond its initial purpose and finding increased acceptance in business and scientific applications.

Pasal is well suited for both batch and interactive modes, although most Pascal business applications are batch-oriented.

Pascal receives avid support from its users because, while it is relatively easy to learn (like BASIC), it is powerful (like PL/I). Unlike PL/I, Pascal is available on microcomputers and seems to be a good alternative to BASIC for use on small computers.

Perhaps the major disadvantage of Pascal is that it is not yet standardized. Many versions and enhancements are available from manufacturers, which means that programs written in Pascal may differ, depending on the specific compiler used. In addition, some people believe that Pascal has poor input/output capabilities. Figure 3–8 shows the payroll program in Pascal.

APL. **APL** (*A Programming Language*) is also well suited for interactive computing. It has a small number of basic operations that can be combined to form many powerful functions. Conceived in 1962 by Kenneth Iverson, APL became available to the public through IBM in 1968 and, over the years, has been expanded.

APL can perform some very complex operations with a minimum of coding. APL's lack of formal restrictions on input and output and its free-form style make it a very powerful language. APL is also available through timesharing networks for organizations that need only a limited amount of data processing.

APL has a few disadvantages as well. It is very difficult to read. A special keyboard is required to enter APL statements; fortunately, however, the larger offering of new, low-cost terminals capable of handling several type styles has greatly reduced this problem. Another limitation of APL is the large amount of primary storage required by its compiler. Figure 3–9 shows an interactive APL session.

Obviously, programming languages were designed for different programming situations. Since businesses have a wide variety of processing needs, they may elect to use several languages to meet their requirements. Table 3–1 shows a comparison among all the languages discussed here.

STEPS IN THE
PROGRAMMING PROCESS

When programs were first written, few rules existed for programmers to follow because there were few things computers could do. Today, however, with the vast array of programming languages, processing techniques, storage devices, and printing media, a programmer is well advised to use a structured approach to problem solving and program development. Four steps have been found helpful in this process: (1) defining the problem, (2) designing a solution, (3) writing the program, and (4) compiling, debugging, and testing the program.

FIGURE 3–8 Payroll Program in Pascal

```
PROGRAM PAYROLL (INPUT,OUTPUT);
VAR HOURS,REGULAR,WAGE,OVERTIME,GROSS,TAX,NETPAY : REAL;
NAME : ARRAY(.1..17.) OF CHAR;
I : INTEGER;
BEGIN
WRITELN('1','EMPLOYEE NAME','                  NET PAY');
WRITELN('   ');
WHILE NOT EOF DO
   BEGIN
   FOR I:=1 TO 17 DO
      READ (NAME(.I.));
      READLN (HOURS,WAGE);
      IF HOURS> 40
         THEN BEGIN
            REGULAR:=40*WAGE;
            OVERTIME:=(HOURS-40)*(1.5*WAGE);
            GROSS:=REGULAR + OVERTIME
         END
         ELSE BEGIN
            GROSS:=HOURS*WAGE
         END;
      IF GROSS>250
         THEN BEGIN
            TAX:=0.20*GROSS;
            NETPAY:=GROSS-TAX
         END
         ELSE BEGIN
            TAX:=0.14*GROSS;
            NETPAY:=GROSS-TAX
         END;
   WRITE(' ');
FOR I :=1 TO 17 DO
      WRITE(NAME(.I.));
      WRITELN(NETPAY:12:12);
   END
END.
```

Output

```
EMPLOYEE NAME    NET PAY

LYNN MANGINO     224.00
THOMAS RITTER    212.42
MARIE OLSON      209.00
LORI DUNLEVY     172.00
WILLIAM WILSON   308.00
```

FIGURE 3–9 Interactive APL Session

```
      ∇PALINDROME[□]∇

    ∇ PALINDROME PHRASE;ALPHA;COMPRESSED;REVERSE
[1]   ⍝  PROGRAM TO DETERMINE IF A PHRASE IS A PALINDROME
[2]   ⍝  THE PHRASE MUST BE CHARACTER DATA AND HAVE AT LEAST ONE
[3]   ALPHA←'ABCDEFGHIJKLMNOPQRSTUVWXYZ'
[4]   COMPRESSED←(PHRASE∈ALPHA)/PHRASE
[5]   →(0 =ρCOMPRESSED)/NONE
[6]   REVERSE←COMPRESSED[⍎⍳ρCOMPRESSED]
[7]   →( ∧/REVERSE=COMPRESSED)/YES
[8]   PHRASE,'  IS NOT A PALINDROME'
[9]   →0
[10] YES:PHRASE,'  IS A PALINDROME'
[11]  →0
[12] NONE:'THERE ARE NO ALPHABETIC CHARACTER IN PHRASE'
    ∇


      PALINDROME 'MOM'
MOM  IS A PALINDROME


      PALINDROME 'THIS'
THIS  IS NOT A PALINDROME


      PALINDROME 'MADAM IN EDEN I''M ADAM'
MADAM IN EDEN I'M ADAM  IS A PALINDROME


      PALINDROME '1 21 '
THERE ARE NO ALPHABETIC CHARACTER IN PHRASE
```

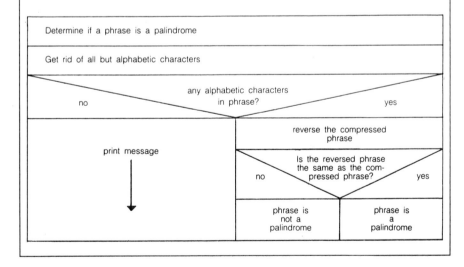

TABLE 3-1 Comparison of Programming Languages

	ASSEMBLY LANGUAGE	FORTRAN	COBOL	PL/I	RPG	BASIC	PASCAL	APL
Strong math capabilities	X	X		X		X	X	X
Good character-manipulation capabilities	X		X	X		X	X	X
English-like			X	X			X	
Available on many computers	X	X	X		X	X	X	
Highly efficient	X							
Standardized		X	X	X		X		
Requires large amount of storage			X	X				X
Good interactive capability						X	X	X
Procedure-oriented		X	X	X		X	X	X
Problem-oriented					X			
Machine-dependent	X							

Defining the Problem

The first step in defining a problem begins with recognizing a need for information. This need may be expressed as a request from management, users, or from a system analyst performing a system study. The analyst/programmer receiving the request must analyze the problem thoroughly in order to understand what is required to solve it. One method used to define the problem analyzes the input, processing, and output required.

When the output that is required of the program is defined, the information needs of users and management become clear. The analyst/programmer often prepares report mock-ups to show users, and asks them to verify the output requirements. In this way, the analyst/programmer can quickly determine whether any omissions or incorrect assumptions about the purpose of the program were made.

Next, the input required to provide this output must be determined. The analyst/programmer reviews current systems to see what data is available and to determine what new data items must be captured in order to provide the required information.

Finally, given (1) the output specifications developed by the analyst/programmer in close cooperation with the users and management and (2) the required input established by careful evaluation of the current systems, the processing requirements can be determined. Once they are known, the analyst/programmer proceeds to the next step—planning a solution.

Designing a Solution

A program, as discussed earlier, is a set of instructions used by the computer to solve a problem. The programmer takes each of the processing segments uncovered in the definition step and works out a tentative program flow; that is, what needs to be done first in the program, what second, and so on. By approaching each segment separately, the programmer can concentrate on developing an efficient and logical flow for that segment.

Basic Logic Patterns   The computer can understand and execute only four basic logic patterns: simple sequence, selection, loop, and branch. Higher-level languages may have more complicated statements, but they all are based on these four patterns (Figure 3–10).

Simple Sequence.   **Simple sequence** logic involves the computer's executing one statement after another in the order given by the programmer. It is the most simple and often-used pattern; in fact, the computer assumes that all statements entered by the programmer are to be executed in this fashion unless it is told otherwise.

Selection.   The **selection** pattern requires that the computer make a choice. Each selection is made on the basis of a comparison that determines whether one item is equal to, less than, or greater than another. In fact, these are the only comparisons the computer can make. Complex selections are made by the use of a sequence of these comparisons.

Loop.   The loop pattern enables the programmer to instruct the computer to loop back to a previous statement in the program. The computer then reexecutes statements according to the simple sequence flow.

Branch.   The last and most controversial pattern is the branch. The **branch** is most efficiently used in combination with selection or looping. This pattern allows the programmer to skip past statements in a program, leaving them unexecuted.

Branching is controversial for several reasons. If a program uses it too often, the computer must frequently jump from one part of the program to another. It is extremely difficult, if not impossible, for one programmer to understand another's program when branching is used too often. Such programs are also difficult and time consuming to update or change. Structured programming, which seeks to reduce the use of branching techniques, will be discussed shortly.

Techniques   Obviously, the solution of a program must be well thought out before programming is started. The problem must be stated in such a way that it can be solved by the use of a series of simple sequence instructions, selections, loops, and in some cases, branches. Even the selections have to be simplified so that they involve only equal-to, less-than, or greater-than comparisons.

When faced with the task of writing a series of programs designed to solve complicated problems, the programmer can easily make omissions and errors in processing logic. Pseudocode and flowchart techniques can help the programmer avoid such omissions and errors.

FIGURE 3–10 Four Traditional Program-Logic Patterns

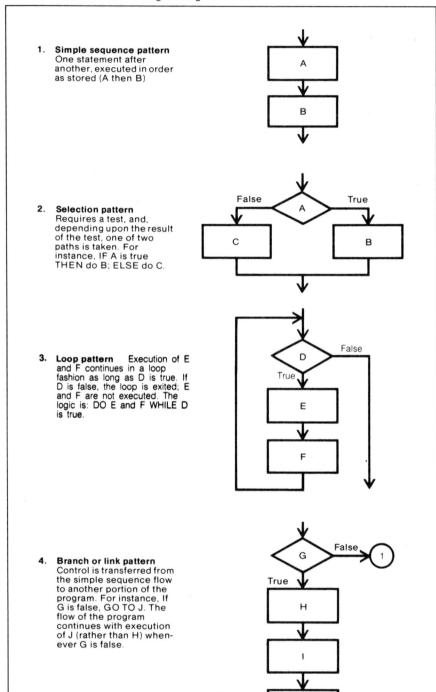

1. **Simple sequence pattern**
   One statement after another, executed in order as stored (A then B)

2. **Selection pattern**
   Requires a test, and, depending upon the result of the test, one of two paths is taken. For instance, IF A is true THEN do B; ELSE do C.

3. **Loop pattern** Execution of E and F continues in a loop fashion as long as D is true. If D is false, the loop is exited; E and F are not executed. The logic is: DO E and F WHILE D is true.

4. **Branch or link pattern**
   Control is transferred from the simple sequence flow to another portion of the program. For instance, If G is false, GO TO J. The flow of the program continues with execution of J (rather than H) whenever G is false.

Pseudocode. **Pseudocode** can be thought of as a narrative description of the processing steps to be performed in a program. The programmer arranges these descriptions in the same order that the program statements will appear in the program. Pseudocoding allows the programmer to focus on the steps needed to perform a particular process, without necessarily worrying about the requirements of a particular computer language. Figure 3–11 is an example of pseudocode used to describe the processing steps required to calculate a shopper's grocery bill. Notice in the figure how the logic patterns just discussed are expressed.

Flowcharts. A **flowchart,** sometimes called a **block diagram,** provides a visual frame of reference for the processing steps in a program. Instead of using the English-like statements of pseudocode, flowcharting uses easily recognizable symbols to represent the type of processing performed in a program. These symbols are arranged in the same logical sequence in which corresponding program statements will appear in the program. Figure 3–12 shows the pseudocode example in flowchart form.

Notice that a flowchart begins at the top of the page and usually is read from top to bottom or left to right. All flowchart blocks must have a verbal explanation that is both understandable and concise. Use of a personal shorthand that is not recognizable by others should be avoided; it makes the diagram confusing.

Flowcharts provide excellent documentation of a program. For maintenance, the flowchart can be used to guide the programmer in determining what statements are required in order to make any necessary changes, and where to locate them. Once the flowchart is updated to reflect these changes, it provides good documentation of the revised program.

The American National Standards Institute (ANSI) has adopted a set of flowchart symbols that is commonly accepted and used by programmers. Figure 3–13 shows some of the ANSI flowchart symbols.

Structured Programming. Emphasis on the art of programming and on the flexibility that high-level languages provide has sometimes en-

FIGURE 3–11 Example of Pseudocode

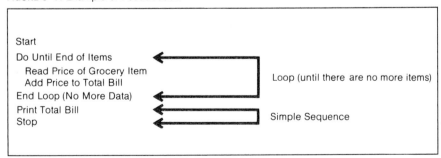

FIGURE 3–12 Example of a Flowchart

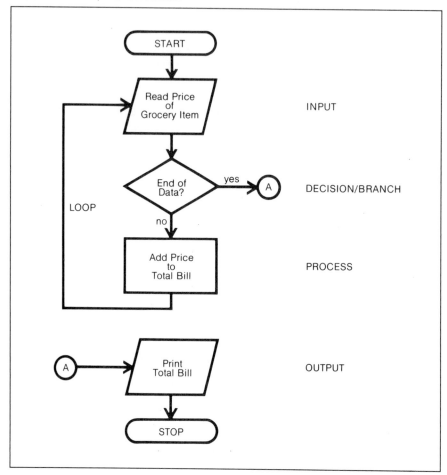

couraged poor programming techniques. For example, many programs contain numerous branches that continually alter the sequential flow of processing. These programs may seem to work successfully, but their often confusing logic can be understood only by the original programmer. This increases the costs and difficulties associated with program maintenance. Furthermore, without a standardized method of attacking a problem, a programmer may spend far more time than necessary in determining an appropriate solution and developing the program. So that these tendencies can be countered, **structured programming** has been widely publicized.

Structured programming has four objectives:

1. To reduce testing time and to increase assurance of program correctness.

2. To increase programmer productivity.

FIGURE 3–13 Flowchart Symbols

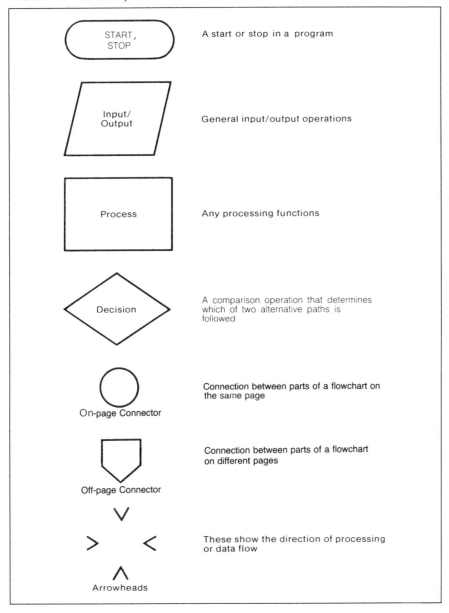

3. To increase clarity by reducing complexity.

4. To decrease maintenance time and effort.

In other words, programs should be easy to read, easy to maintain, and easy to change.

Structured programming encourages well-thought-out program logic and suggests using only three basic control patterns: simple sequence, selection, and loop (see earlier discussion). With these three patterns, programs can be read from top to bottom and are easier to understand. An attempt is made to keep programs as simple and straightforward as possible.

Basic to the concept of structured programming is the use of program modules. Each module is an independent program segment that performs only one function. These modules can be coded and combined to form the complete program. This **top-down approach** signifies program maintenance, since necessary changes can be isolated to the appropriate module and the rest of the program can often remain unchanged.

Modules should be small in order to facilitate programming and later corrections. Each module should have only one entry point and one exit point. This allows the flow of control to be followed easily by the programmer. When the modular approach is used, the one-entry/ one-exit guideline is easy to incorporate into the program. A program that has only one entrance and one exit is called a **proper program.**

Structured programs are characterized by other special features. Comments, statements, or remarks should be used liberally. Variable names should be definite. Finally, indentation and spacing of program statements should be used.

It must be emphasized that the branch pattern, characterized by the GO TO statement, is not advocated in structured programming. (In fact, structured programming is sometimes called "GO-TO-less" programming or "IF-THEN-ELSE" programming.) A GO TO statement causes an unconditional branch to exist from one part of the program to another. Excessive use of GO TO statements results in continual changes in the flow of execution. Often the flow is transferred to totally different logical sections of the program. Programs containing many GO TO (branching) statements are difficult to modify because they are obscure and complicated. A programmer may not know how a change in one part of the program will affect processing in other parts. This is not to say that a structured program will not have any GO TO statements, but that they should never cause a branch to exist outside of the program module in which they reside.

Some programming languages are better suited to structured programming than others. Especially well suited are Pascal, PL/I, and ALGOL (a language developed by a cooordinated effort of user groups in Europe). Languages such as FORTRAN and BASIC lack some features that many people consider essential for structured programming. For example, it is difficult to avoid the use of GO TO statements in these languages. However, careful planning and well-placed GO TO statements can result in well-structured programs, regardless of the language used.

HIPO.   A graphical technique for illustrating program logic that is often used in conjunction with structured programming is **HIPO** (*Hi-*

erarchy plus Input, Processing, and Output). A HIPO chart describes a program as a hierarchical arrangement of functions to be performed. In keeping with the structured-programming philosophy, HIPO emphasizes the modular construction of the program that is to be written.

In HIPO, the program structure is diagrammed on paper, with the major task at the top and individual subtasks beneath it. From left to right on the chart, the main functions of input, processing, and output appear in order. From top to bottom, functions are defined as an increasingly more specific set of tasks. HIPO is not a flowchart, however. Flowcharts emphasize the step-by-step logical sequence of a program. HIPO deals instead with the structure of the program, usually in more general terms than a flowchart would. In fact, flowcharts are frequently used with HIPO to chart in detail the logic contained within the various HIPO modules.

A HIPO chart used to diagram a specific problem is illustrated in Figure 3–14. A program is to be written to process inventory. Input for the program will consist of current transactions in the form of sales tickets and a data file containing relevant information about the firm's inventory. After the data has been read, the program will use the input to compute current inventory levels. It will also keep track of those items of inventory falling below predetermined minimum levels. (These levels are found in the inventory master file.) The program will then generate a new, updated master file and print a listing of inventory items that should be reordered.

Decision-Logic Tables. A final method of organizing a problem solution is through the use of a **decision-logic table (DLT).** A DLT is a standardized, verbally-oriented table that allows the programmer to list all the decisions and actions to be made in solving a problem. It is divided into four parts that serve distinct purposes (Figure 3–15).

Part A: **Condition stub**—questions all factors that need to be considered in determining a course of action; covers all conditions listed in the problem.

Part B: **Action stub**—describes all actions that are applicable to the problem.

Part C: **Condition entry**—answers all questions in the condition stub.

Part D: **Action entry**—specifies which actions should be taken.

The development of a logical solution to a complex problem is difficult and confusing unless a systematic approach is used to analyze the problem. Decision-logic tables are a technique for organizing relevant facts in a clear and concise manner. DLTs are often used in con-

FIGURE 3–14 HIPO Function Chart for Sample Case

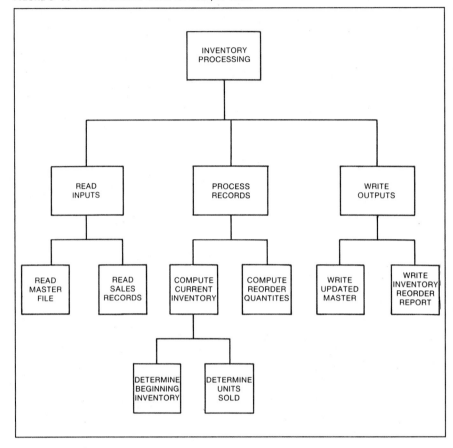

junction with flowcharts to delineate certain segments of logic that are easier to present in DLT format.

Figure 3–16 shows a DLT used in conjunction with a customer-billing application. A firm has two classes of customers. Retail customers are charged the regular prices for orders. Wholesale customers are charged discounted prices. In addition, either a full or a partial order may be shipped to a customer, depending on the availability of inventory. As the example shows, four different courses of action are possible for each order, depending on the combination of conditions present. A DLT aids the programmer in considering all conditions and actions associated with a specific problem.

Writing the Program

After the programmer has defined the problem and designed a solution, the program is written in a specific programming language. Program-

FIGURE 3–15 Decision-Logic Table

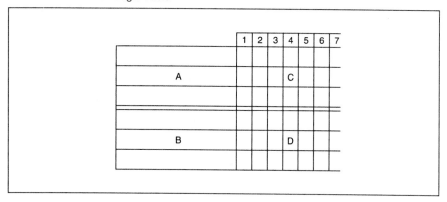

ming languages are usually designed for specific types of applications. A programmer may have no part in the selection of a language for a particular application—there may be a business requirement to use COBOL, for instance, because of its readability.

Desirable Program Qualities As the program is being coded, the programmer should be aware that generating the correct output is not the only requirement of a good program. More than one way can be found to code a program to provide the correct solution; however, one program can be better than another. The programmer should try to incorporate the following qualities into any program:

Programs should be easy to read and understand. Data names should be descriptive. Statements should be placed in a format that is easy to follow. In other words, the programmer should write the program in such a way that someone else can easily read and understand it.

Programs should be reliable. They should consistently produce the correct output. All formulas and computations, as well as logic tests and transfers of control, must be accurate.

FIGURE 3–16 DLT Example

	1	2	3	4
RETAIL CUSTOMER	Y	Y	N	N
WHOLESALE CUSTOMER	N	N	Y	Y
QTY ORDERED ≥ STOCK ON HAND	Y	N	Y	N
BILL AT REGULAR PRICE	X	X		
BILL AT DISCOUNT PRICE			X	X
SHIP COMPLETE ORDER	X		X	
SHIP PARTIAL AND BACKORDER SHORTAGE		X		X

Programs should work under all conditions. Reliability alone is no guarantee of a successful program. Internal logic may be correct, but an incorrect data item (garbage in) could produce incorrect output (garbage out). For example, a program that uses the age of a person may want to test for incorrect ages in the data stream. How would the program react if someone's age were 4,692 or −35?

Programs should be maintainable. They should be easy to update and modify. Programs should be written in independent segments so that a change in one segment does not necessitate a change in others.

Compiling, Debugging, and Testing
the Program

Language Translation   Assembly and high-level languages are much more widely used by programmers than machine language. Since these languages cannot be executed directly by computers, they are converted into machine-executable form by the language-translator program, as described earlier. The machine-language form of the program, the object program, accomplishes the same operations as a program originally written in machine language. Compilers are designed for specific machines and languages. For example, a compiler that translates a source program written in FORTRAN into a machine-language program could not translate COBOL statements (Figure 3–17).

During the compilation or assembly (the translation process), the object program is generated. The programmer receives a source-program listing that indicates any errors detected during translation. The

FIGURE 3–17 One COBOL Statement and Corresponding Machine-Language Instructions

```
(a) COBOL

STANDARD-ROUTINE.
   MULTIPLY HOURS-WORKED BY WAGE-PER-HOUR GIVING GROSS PAY.


(b) MACHINE LANGUAGE

*STANDARD-ROUTINE
          000778
MULTIPLY  000778  F2  71  D  1E8  7  010
          00077E  F2  73  D  1F0  7  012
          000784  FC  42  D  1EB  D  1E5
          00078A  F3  43  6  000  D  1EC
          000790  96  F0  6  004
          000794  58  10  D  21C
          000798  07  F1
```

errors are usually violations of the rules associated with the particular programming language, and they are called **syntax** errors. For example, if a statement that should begin in column 8 begins in column 6, an error message will be generated. Similarly, an error message will be generated if language keywords such as WRITE or COMPUTE are misspelled.

The compiler can provide a listing of all compiler-detected errors. This error-message listing may give the number of each statement in error and may also describe the nature of the error (Figure 3–18). Only after all detected errors have been corrected can the object program be submitted to the computer for execution. Several attempts at successful compilation or assembly may be needed.

Debugging the Program   The compiler that translates the program can detect grammatical errors, such as misspellings and incorrect punctuation. However, logical errors are often harder to detect. Such errors may result when the programmer does not fully understand the problem or does not account for problems that may arise during processing.

An error in a program has acquired the nickname **bug** because a problem with the Mark II computer in 1945 was actually a moth caught in a relay. The process of locating, isolating, and eliminating bugs is often called **debugging.** The amount of time that must be spent in debugging depends on the quality of the program. However, a newly completed program rarely executes successfully the first time it is run. In fact, one-third to one-half of a programmer's time is spent in debugging.

Testing the Program   Testing a program involves executing it by using input data that is either a representative sample of actual data or a facsimile. Often, sample data that can be manipulated easily by the programmer is used so that the computer-determined output can be compared with programmer-determined correct results. The output

FIGURE 3–18 Compiler-Detected Errors

```
STATEMENT
  NUMBER      ERROR CODE              ERROR MESSAGES
    |             |
  1972        IKF10801-W    PERIOD PRECEDED BY SPACE. ASSUME END OF SENTENCE.
  1999        IKF10801-W    PERIOD PRECEDED BY SPACE. ASSUME END OF SENTENCE.
  2074        IKF10431-W    END OF SENTENCE SHOULD PRECEDE 02. ASSUMED PRESENT.
  2399        IKF21261-C    VALUE CLAUSE LITERAL TOO LONG. TRUNCATED TO PICTURE SIZE.
  2432        IKF10431-W    END OF SENTENCE SHOULD PRECEDE 02. ASSUMED PRESENT.
  2481        IKF10801-W    PERIOD PRECEDED BY SPACE. ASSUME END OF SENTENCE.
  2464        IKF10801-W    PERIOD PRECEDED BY SPACE. ASSUME END OF SENTENCE.
  2623        IKF10041-E    INVALID WORD NOTE. SKIPPING TO NEXT RECOGNIZABLE WORD.
  2623        IKF10071-W    MINUS SIGN NOT PRECEDED BY A SPACE. ASSUME SPACE.
  2623        IKF10071-W    **NOT PRECEDED BY A SPACE. ASSUME SPACE.
```

should be easy to recognize so that the programmer can see whether it is correct.

A complex program is frequently tested in separate units so that errors can be isolated to specific sections, helping to narrow the search for the cause of an error. The programmer must correct all mistakes; running and rerunning a specific unit may be necessary before the cause of an error can be found. The programmer then rewrites the part in error and resubmits it for another test. Care must be taken so that correction of one logical error does not give rise to several others.

Each section of the program must be tested (even sections that will be used infrequently). If instructions for handling exceptions are part of the program, the sample input data should include items that test the program's ability to spot and reject improper data items. The programmer often finds **desk-checking** (desk-debugging) helpful. With this method, the programmer pretends to be the computer and, reading each instruction and simulating how the computer would process a data item, attempts to catch any flaws in the program logic.

After a programmer has worked for a long time to correct the logic of a program, he or she may tend to overlook errors or assume a clarity that in reality does not exist. For this reason, programmers sometimes trade their partially debugged programs among themselves. The programmer examining a "fresh" program may uncover mistakes in logic that were unnoticed by the original programmer.

Programming Case Study

Defining the Problem   The problem we will examine and program is to calculate students' final grades for a class. Once the teacher has assigned a grade for each test given in the class, the computer is to calculate a student's numerical average for all tests, and then assign a letter-grade equivalent.

Designing a Solution   The first step in designing a solution is to determine what output is required of the program. The teacher would like each student's name, the average test score, and the letter-grade equivalent. The input to the program will be each student's name and five test scores. The **processing** required of the program will be to add together the five scores, divide by five (the number of tests) to calculate the average, and then assign a letter grade. Letter grades will be assigned on the basis of the following scale:

Average	Final Grade
90–100	A
80–89	B
70–79	C
60–69	D
0–59	F

The next step in designing a problem solution is to determine a basic instruction flow. Output headings can be printed before the student data is read as input. Since each student has five grades, the student's name and five grades must be input, and the grades added together. When the addition has been completed, the average can be calculated. Once the average has been determined, the appropriate final letter grade can be assigned according to the grade scale. After the final letter grade has been established, the name, average, and final grade can be printed. When the data for one student has been processed, the data for the next student can be read and processed, and so on, until no more statistics are available.

The flow can be placed into steps as follows:

1. Print headings.

2. If all students have not been processed, do steps 3 through 8, otherwise go to step 9.

3. Read student's name and five grades.

4. Total the student's numerical grades.

5. Calculate the student's grade average.

6. Determine the final letter grade based on the grade scale.

7. Print name, average, and final letter grade.

8. Go back to step 2.

9. Print message signifying end of the program.

10. Stop.

A flowchart for the solution of this problem is given in Figure 3–19. The relationship between the steps just outlined and the blocks on the flowchart is also pointed out.

Writing the Program   After the flowchart has been constructed and the logic reviewed, the next task is to express the solution in a programming language—in this case, BASIC. The completed source program can then be entered into the computer by the programmer. Figure 3–20 shows the source listing for the program.

Compiling, Debugging, and Testing the Program   Once the program has been written, it can be submitted to the computer in order to be compiled into machine language. A listing of the source program and notification of errors (if any) detected by the computer can be generated. Then the program can be executed. Figure 3–21 shows the output produced during the execution of the program.

FIGURE 3–19 Flowchart for Case Study

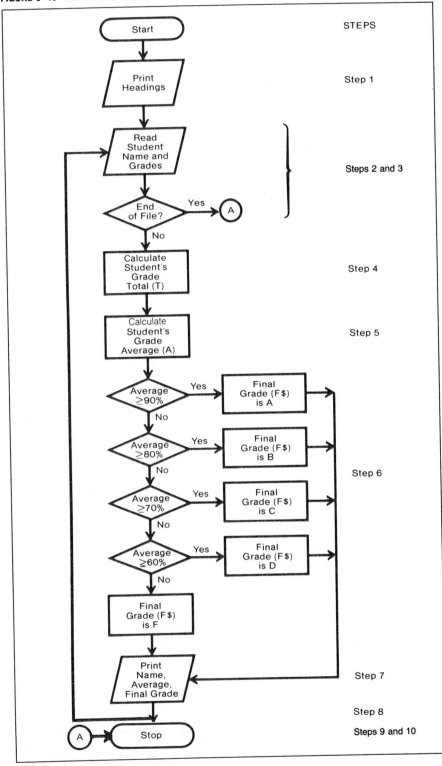

FIGURE 3-20 BASIC Program with Sample Data for Case Study

```
GRADE    21:54    TUESDAY JULY 27, 1982

100 REM THIS PROGRAM WILL ADD 5 INDIVIDUAL GRADES
110 REM FOR A STUDENT, CALCULATE THE AVERAGE, AND THEN
120 REM DETERMINE THE STUDENT'S FINAL GRADE
130 PRINT 'NAME', 'AVERAGE', 'FINAL GRADE'
140 PRINT
150 READ N$, G1, G2, G3, G4, G5
155 IF N$ = 'END OF DATA' THEN 997
160 LET T = G1+G2+G3+G4+G5
170 LET A = T/5
180 IF A >= 90 THEN 240
190 IF A >= 80 THEN 260
200 IF A >= 70 THEN 280
210 IF A >= 60 THEN 300.
220 LET F$ = 'F'
230 GO TO 310
240 LET F$ = 'A'
250 GO TO 310
260 LET F$ = 'B'
270 GO TO 310
280 LET F$ = 'C'
290 GO TO 310
300 LET F$ = 'D'
310 PRINT N$, A, F$
320 GO TO 150
330 DATA 'FRED J. SMITH', 70, 65, 24, 100, 98
340 DATA 'JASON R. JACKSON', 97, 96, 59, 78, 60
350 DATA 'JOHN S. LAWSON', 90, 94, 88, 98, 96
360 DATA 'SUSAN EAKINS', 83, 76, 87, 89, 95
370 DATA 'MARY Q. JOHNSON', 66, 79, 83, 75, 70
380 DATA 'END OF DATA', 0, 0, 0, 0, 0
997 PRINT 'END OF PROGRAM'
998 STOP
999 END
```

SOFTWARE PACKAGES

With the development of operating-system programs, interest in the commercial aspect of program development has gained in importance. Since the early 1970s, advances in programming have been considered as important as improvements in equipment. A **software package** is a set of standardized computer programs, procedures, and related documentation necessary to solve problems of a specific application; examples are an inventory control package and a statistical analysis package.

Many organizations employ their own programmers to develop programs for internal operations. This is called **in-house development,** and

FIGURE 3–21 Output for Case Study

```
RUN GRADE

GRADE      21:54    TUESDAY JULY 27, 1982

NAME                      AVERAGE          FINAL GRADE

FRED J. SMITH             71.4                C
JASON R. JACKSON          78                  C
JOHN S. LAWSON            93.2                A
SUSAN EAKINS              86                  B
MARY Q. JOHNSON           74.6                C
END OF PROGRAM
```

it allows for programming creativity while satisfying customer/user requirements. However, this approach requires significant expenditures for staff. In addition, many other organizations may be writing programs to accomplish the same basic objectives (often reinventing the wheel). Because of these disadvantages, interest groups have been created for the purpose of sharing software among organizations operating in similar environments.

Many firms specializing in software development have been formed to meet the growing demand for prewritten programs. Software and consulting activities are requiring an ever-increasing share of data-processing expenditures, thereby reducing the proportion spent on hardware. Although computer manufacturers can supply these services (often at a separate cost), a large market exists for externally supplied computer services.

A **proprietary software package** is a program developed and owned by an organization but sold or leased to many users. When such a package exists and fits a user's requirements (or can be easily adapted to meet such requirements), the price of the package is almost certainly less than that of in-house development. Furthermore, such packages are generally debugged and documented, and ongoing maintenance and support are usually guaranteed. Many packages are also machine-independent, which means they can be used on several types of computer systems. After comparing internal requirements with package capabilities, user management can determine whether it would be cost-effective to proceed with in-house development.

Just as applications programs have become more sophisticated over the years, so have system programs. Early computer systems were plagued by inefficient use of computer resources, either because human intervention was required or because system programs were not sophisticated enough to allocate resources well. Several software developments have come about that greatly increase the overall efficiency of the computer.

Multiprogramming

When the CPU is very active, the system as a whole is more efficient. However, the CPU frequently must remain idle because input/output devices are not fast enough. The CPU can operate on only one instruction at a time; furthermore, it cannot operate on data that is not in primary storage. If an input device is slow in providing data or instructions, the CPU must wait until input/output operations have been completed before executing a program.

Multiprogramming increases CPU active time by effectively allocating computer resources and offsetting low input/output speeds. Under multiprogramming, several programs reside in the primary-storage unit at the same time. Although the CPU can execute only one instruction at a time, it can execute instructions from one program, then another, then another, and back to the first again. Instructions from one program are executed until an interrupt for either input or output is generated. While the input/output operation takes place, the CPU can shift its attention to another program in memory. The computer executes the second program until it, too, requires input or output. This rotation occurs so quickly that the execution of the programs in storage appears to be simultaneous. More precisely, the CPU executes the different programs concurrently, which means "over the same period of time."

Virtual Storage

Multiprogramming increases system efficiency because the CPU can concurrently execute programs instead of waiting while input/output operations occur. A limitation of multiprogramming, however, is that all the instructions of a program are kept in primary storage throughout its execution, whether they are needed or not. Yet, a large program may contain many sequences of instructions that are executed infrequently. As processing requirements increase, the physical limitation of memory becomes a critical constraint, and the productive use of memory becomes increasingly important.

So that this problem could be alleviated, an extension of multiprogramming called **virtual storage** has been developed on the principle that only a portion of a program (that portion needed immediately) has to be in primary storage at any given time. The rest of the program and data can be kept in auxiliary storage. Since only part of a program is in primary storage, more programs can be placed there at one time. More programs can be executed within a given time period. This gives the illusion that main storage is unlimited.

To implement virtual storage (or virtual memory, as it is sometimes called), a direct-access storage device such as a magnetic-disk unit is used to augment primary storage. The term **real storage** is usually given to primary storage within the CPU, whereas virtual storage refers to the direct-access storage (Figure 3–22). Both real- and virtual-storage locations are given addresses by the operating system. If data or instructions needed are not in the real (primary) storage area, the portion of the program containing them is transferred from virtual storage into real storage, while another portion currently in real storage may be written back to virtual storage (or merely overlaid in primary storage). This process is known as **swapping.**

One of the major limitations of virtual storage is the requirement for extensive online auxiliary storage. Also, the virtual-storage operating system itself is highly sophisticated and requires significant amounts of internal storage. If virtual storage is not used wisely, much time can be spent swapping portions of a program in and out of real storage. Very little processing occurs compared with the amount of swapping. This is known as **thrashing.**

Multiprocessing

Multiprocessing involves the use of two or more central processing units linked together for coordinated operation. Stored-program instructions are executed simultaneously, but by different CPUs. The CPUs may execute different instructions from the same program, or they may execute totally different programs. (In contrast, under multiprogramming,

FIGURE 3–22 Schematic Drawing of Virtual Storage and Swapping

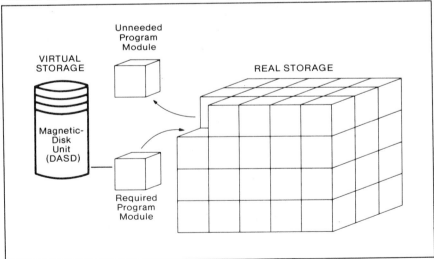

the computer appears to be processing different jobs simultaneously, but is actually processing them concurrently.)

Coordinating the efforts of several CPUs requires highly sophisticated software and careful planning. The scheduling of workloads for the CPUs involves making the most efficient use of computer resources. Implementing such a system is a time-consuming endeavor that may require the services of outside consultants as well as those provided by the equipment manufacturers. The payoff from this effort is a system with capabilities extending far beyond those of a single-CPU system.

————————————————— SUMMARY —————————————————

● A program is a series of step-by-step instructions required to solve a problem. Applications programs solve user problems; system programs coordinate the operation of all computer circuitry.

● An operating system is a collection of system programs designed to permit a computer system to manage its own operations. The supervisor is the major component of the operating system, and it controls the other subsystems: the input/output management system, job-control language, library programs, utility programs, and language translators.

● There are three sets of language groups: (1) machine language, which is a combination of 0s and 1s and is the only language the computer can execute directly; (2) assembly language, which provides convenient symbols and abbreviations for writing programs; and (3) higher-level languages, which are English-like and procedure- and problem-oriented.

● There are four traditional patterns of programming logic that can be used to solve any problem: simple sequence, selection, loop, and branch.

● In solving a problem, a programmer follows four steps: (1) defining the problem, (2) designing a solution, (3) writing the program, and (4) compiling, debugging, and testing the program.

● Development tools are available to help the programmer in the design phase of problem solving—pseudocode and flowcharts. Pseudocode attempts to express in short English phrases the steps the program will take. Flowcharts use standard symbols to visually depict the logical processes within the program.

● In designing a solution, the programmer must make special considerations with regard to input, processing, and output. The method of input, type of edit checks, and form of output will affect how a program should be designed.

● HIPO is a method of graphically describing a system or program as an arrangement of functions to be performed.

—————————— REVIEW QUESTIONS ——————————

1. The basic pattern known as the "do-while" pattern is the
   a. link.
   b. loop.
   c. selection.
   d. simple sequence.

2. A popular English-like description of the processing steps in a program is
   a. quasicode.
   b. pseudocode.
   c. trailer values.
   d. flowcharts.

3. The term *software* is used to describe
   a. electrical circuitry.
   b. all computer programs.
   c. punched cards and magnetic tape.
   d. all input/output devices.

4. A language-translator program transforms source-program statements into
   a. higher-level language.
   b. job-control language.
   c. a compiler.
   d. an object program.

5. Structured programming tries to eliminate the _____ pattern, which has GO TO statements inherent in it.
   a. simple-sequence
   b. selection
   c. loop
   d. branch

6. To get an assembly-language or a higher-level-language program into machine-executable form requires a(n)
   a. translator program.
   b. machine-language program.
   c. object program.
   d. utility program.

7. Which of the following statements about multiprogramming is false?

    a. Several programs are resident in the primary-storage unit at once.

    b. Execution of programs appears to be simultaneous.

    c. Programs must be kept separate.

    d. The control unit of the CPU processes more than one instruction at a time.

8. The linkage editor performs which of the following tasks?

    a. Generates an object program.

    b. Assigns the program an address.

    c. Edits and formats the object program.

    d. Both (b) and (c).

9. The communication link between the programmer and the operating system is

    a. the compiler.

    b. the job-control program.

    c. a utility program.

    d. the channel.

10. Syntax errors are most frequently discovered during which of the following error-checking procedures?

    a. Compilation

    b. Debugging

    c. Desk-checking

    d. Test data runs

11. Which of the following items are contained in a decision table?

    a. Conditions

    b. Actions

    c. Yes and no to questions

    d. All of the above

12. Which of the following is the only language the computer can execute directly?

    a. APL

    b. Assembly language

    c. Machine language

    d. BASIC

13. Multiprocessing uses multiple

    a. CPUs linked together.

    b. programs and swapping.

    c. programmers using structured-programming techniques.

    d. thrashing.

14. Virtual storage
    a. is not used by many organizations because it requires a great extension of secondary storage.
    b. means that primary memory is underused.
    c. gives the impression that primary-storage capacity is increased although it really is not.
    d. is used for customer-credit processing.

15. Which of the following programming languages is best known for its file-manipulation capabilities?
    a. RPG
    b. BASIC
    c. FORTRAN
    d. COBOL

16. The term *higher-level languages* comes from the fact that
    a. the machines the languages run on are highly sophisticated.
    b. the languages display a higher level of machine orientation.
    c. the languages are the farthest removed from the hardware.
    d. the languages were created at a later date than other languages.

17. The efficiency of a computer system is determined primarily by how much time the _____ is(are) kept busy with useful work.
    a. operating system
    b. channels
    c. input/output devices
    d. CPU

18. Structured programming
    a. tries to do away with the branch pattern.
    b. has an objective of reducing the complexity of a program.
    c. decreases the time a programmer must devote to debugging and desk-checking.
    d. is all of the above.

19. An example of an applications program is
    a. a program used for inventory control.
    b. a program that determines job priorities within the computer.
    c. a demand-report program.
    d. both (a) and (c).

20. Which of the following is the major component of the operating system?
    a. Job-control language
    b. I/O management system
    c. Monitor program
    d. Library program

COMPUTER SYSTEMS

A **system** is a set of interrelated parts—equipment, procedures, and personnel—that work together to achieve an overall objective. An **information system** is an integrated network designed to satisfy the information requirements of management. Every organization has a method of transferring information from one person to another, whether it is by memo, by letter, or by computer printout. Some information systems are computerized and some are manual.

Several reasons can make management want to review its present information system. Among them are:

1. The system is not functioning properly.

2. A new aspect, such as a new product or procedure, has been added.

3. A new development in system technology has been proposed.

4. The organization wants to update the entire system.

SYSTEM LIFE CYCLE
System Analysis

The investigation process is known as **system analysis.** It is the first phase of the **system life cycle.** A statement of objectives is essential to the identification of information requirements. An information **system analyst** conducts preliminary interviews with users of the present system. By bringing the users' problems into focus, the analyst can determine what information is needed, when it is required, and how it will be used.

A detailed study of the processes the organization uses to manipulate its data must then be performed. By examining the present system, the analyst can determine whether it needs to be altered, restructured, or replaced. If the system is shown to be adequate, the analysis process ends. But if the study shows that changes are in order, the investigation of the organization's requirements continues.

The information system analyst acts as an interface between current and/or proposed users of the information system and technical persons, such as computer programmers and operators. The analyst needs a background in organization operations in order to be able to communicate with the users, and a knowledge of computer technology in order to be able to estimate development and operation costs. Some general considerations must be recognized:

1. Is the input to the system obtained and processed as efficiently and inexpensively as possible?

2. Is the information provided by the system in a form suitable for user decision-making?

3. Is the information complete, correct, and precise?

4. Is the information ready when users need it?

5. Is there an information overload?

System Design

After the analysis is completed, **system design** begins. This phase of the system life cycle allows the analyst to be original and creative. The analyst has the task of translating the information requirements identified in the first phase into a feasible and detailed design plan. This involves developing alternative designs, building formal models of these designs, determining the cost effectiveness of the alternatives, and then making recommendations.

When considering alternative designs, the analyst must be aware of conflicting objectives that may be present in the organization. For example, a sales department may want as many models of a product as possible, but the production department may want to limit the varieties of a product. The problems of each functional area should be brought to the attention of top management so that they can be resolved according to the overall goals of the organization.

In designing alternatives, the analyst should include activities such as structuring forms and reports, determining program specifications, creating a data base, organizing clerical procedures, recruiting and training personnel, and instituting process-control measures. The analyst must determine the feasibility of the design alternatives with respect to money, personnel, time, and facilities. The value of an information system to management should exceed the cost associated with the system. If a report costs $20,000 a year to generate but is worth only $14,000 in beneficial information, it should not be included in the system. In analyzing and designing the alternatives, the analyst can use quantitative methods such as sampling or model simulation, as well as qualitative factors such as judgment, common sense, and experience.

After evaluating the system analyst's recommendation, management can do one of three things: approve the recommendation, approve the recommendation with changes (this includes selecting another alternative), or select none of the alternatives. The "do nothing" alternative is always possible. If the design of the recommended system is approved, the analyst proceeds to implement it.

System Implementation

In the implementation stage of the system methodology, the analyst is able to see the transformation of ideas, flowcharts, and narratives into actual processes, flows, and information. **System implementation** is the adoption of the information system developed in the system-design stage. This transition is not performed easily. Detailed programming specifications must be coded in a computer language, debugged, and put into production. Personnel must be trained to use the new system procedures; the system must be thoroughly documented and tested; and a conversion must be made from the old system to the new one.

One of the primary responsibilities of the system analyst is to see that personnel training is provided to the two groups of people who interface with a system. The first group includes the people who develop, operate, and maintain the system. The second group includes the people who use the information generated by the system to support their decision making. Both must be aware of their responsibilities regarding the system's operation and of what they can and cannot expect from it.

One of the most neglected parts of system implementation has been **documentation.** Many systems were developed in the early 1970s with sparse documentation. This presented no problems when the systems were first implemented. Over time, however, changes in the businesses and their information requirements necessitated making system and programming changes. At that point, organizations painfully realized the need to have extensive system documentation. Understanding programs written five to ten years earlier was often difficult. Changes made to them frequently caused errors in other programs. Thus, most organizations have adopted a system-development methodology requiring adequate documentation of both programs and user procedures.

The switch from an old system to a new one is referred to as **conversion.** Conversion involves not only the changes in the mode of processing data but also the changes in equipment and in clerical procedures. Several approaches can be used to accomplish the conversion process.

When **parallel conversion** is used, the new system is operated side-by-side with the old one for some period of time. This may require additional personnel and can be expensive. It does, however, provide for verifying the output of the new system against the proven results of the old one.

Pilot conversion involves converting only a small piece of the business to the new system. Thus, problems can be discovered in the new system while only that small part of the business is affected. These system "bugs" can be corrected before other areas adopt the system.

With **phased conversion,** the old system is gradually replaced by the new one over a period of time. Phased conversion can be used to replace parts of the old system with modules of the new as they are completed. For instance, the new system may require data-recording procedures to be updated, using terminals instead of input forms; the gathered data nevertheless may be input to the previous system's processing programs while new programs are being developed.

Finally, **crash conversion,** sometimes referred to as **direct conversion,** takes place all at once. Crash conversion may be required when fast adoption of a new system is needed or when new procedures are radically different from the old ones. This is a risky conversion method; there is no other system to fall back on should the new one fail.

System Audit and Review

After the conversion process is complete, the analyst must obtain feedback on the system's performance. Frequently, an audit is conducted to evaluate the system's performance in terms of the initial objectives established for it. The evaluation should ask questions like: Does the system perform as planned and deliver the anticipated benefits? Was the system completed on schedule and with the resources estimated? What controls have been established for input, processing, and output of data? Have users been educated about the new system? Is the system accepted by users? As a result of the audit or of user requests, some modification or improvement of the new system may be required.

No matter how flexible or adaptable a system is, however, major changes become necessary over time. When the system has to be redesigned, the entire system cycle—analysis, design, and implementation—must be performed again. Keeping information systems responsive to information needs is a never-ending process, as can be seen in Figure 4–1.

FIGURE 4–1 System Life Cycle

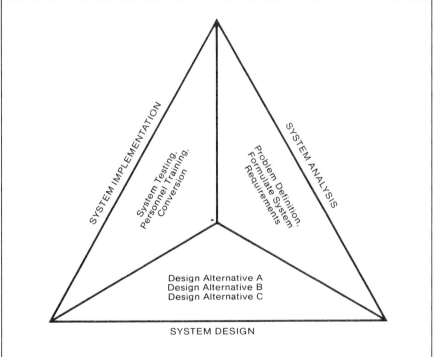

MANAGEMENT INFORMATION
SYSTEMS

Managers have recently recognized that the possibilities for computer use extend beyond normal reporting to include the generation of information to support decision making. This application is known as a **management information system (MIS).** An MIS is a formal information network using computers to provide management with the information it needs to make decisions. The goal of an MIS is to get the correct information to the appropriate manager at the right time.

In considering a management information system, an organization must ensure:

1. Reports on time; if reports are not available when needed, they cannot be used in decision making.

2. Results that the user needs; an MIS cannot be successful if it does not meet the user requirements.

3. Correct information; managers cannot make the best decisions with incorrect data.

4. Room for expansion; as the organization's needs grow, computer capability must be readily available.

Typically, a management information system can generate four kinds of output:

1. **Scheduled listings,** which are received at regular time intervals; this type constitutes the majority of output.

2. **Exception reports,** which monitor performance and indicate deviations from expected results; these are action-oriented management reports.

3. **Predictive reports,** which are used for anticipatory decision making (planning); this allows organizations to project future results based on models.

4. **Demand reports,** which are produced only on request; they are not required on a continuing basis in the total life of the MIS, and they are often requested and displayed through online terminals.

A firm may, for example, organize its inventory files in keeping with the MIS concept. At scheduled intervals, a report that lists inventory in stock is generated. Purchasing managers, sales managers, and accountants, among others, have use for such reports. Report formats are varied according to the special needs of each type of user. Accountants preparing financial statements need much less detail and much more summarization than do purchasing agents, who need detailed reports specific to their own product areas.

In conjunction with scheduled listings, a report that cites problem areas within the inventory can be generated. For example, fast-moving items can be listed so they can be ordered more frequently or in greater quantity. Alternatively, a list of slow-moving items can be generated so management can take steps to cull such items from the inventory. Furthermore, the computer can be programmed to analyze inventory trends. The sales department is interested in information about sales trends, which helps it make decisions about adding and dropping products and product lines. The finance department watches developing trends in inventory costs so it can make provisions for financing future inventory purchases.

Finally, if inventory files are organized on direct-access storage devices, interrogation of inventory files is possible. Salespeople on the road can, for instance, determine exact inventory levels by accessing the files through portable terminals. As these examples illustrate, the MIS attempts to use data files efficiently by making the information contained in them as useful as possible to all authorized, interested individuals.

Although the MIS can assist in developing more effective management, it cannot guarantee decision-making success. One problem that frequently arises is determining what information is needed by management. Decision making is an individual art. Experience, intuition, and chance all affect the decision-making process. In designing a system, the analyst relies on the user when determining information requirements.

Frequently, a manager requests everything the computer can provide. The result can be an overload of information. Instead of assisting the manager, information overload creates the problem of distinguishing what is relevant from what is irrelevant. Many MIS installations offer online facilities that allow managers to interact directly with the computer, requesting only the information pertinent to the decision at hand. This approach is particularly effective in helping managers make decisions that affect current operations in an organization.

After a management information system is installed, managers do not always feel that the change has been beneficial to decision making. Often, the problem is that the people who must use the system were not involved in the analysis and design of it. Management frequently expects totally automatic decisions after implementation of an MIS; it fails to recognize that only routine decisions can be programmed. Examples of routine decisions are ordering purchases when inventory stock goes below a certain point, or scheduling production. Decisions that are dependent on more than quantitative data require human involvement because the computer system has no capability for intuition and experience. The final decision, whether correct or incorrect, rests with a human manager who has these qualities. By making information available, a management information system helps to reduce the uncertainty surrounding the decision-making process.

The future of the MIS depends largely on the attitudes of management. In a very real sense, the success of a system is dependent on user involvement. As routine decisions are taken over by computers, management may become resistant to future changes, either because responsibility for decision making is reduced or because managers fear that the computer will make their positions obsolete. An MIS is more apt to be successful when implemented in an organization that is operating on a sound basis than when used in an organization seeking a miracle.

SYSTEM FLOWCHARTING

Program flowcharting (block diagramming) describes in detailed process blocks the operations to be performed on data. A program flowchart does not usually indicate the form of input (tape, card, disk, or drum) or the form of output (tape, document, disk, card, or drum). For any of these forms, a general input/output symbol is used.

System flowcharting, on the other hand, does not emphasize how processing is done, but it does concentrate on what processing is done in the system. Therefore, a system flowchart emphasizes the flow of data through the entire data-processing system, without describing details of internal computer operations. The generalized input/output symbol used in program flowcharting is not specific enough for system flowcharting. A variety of symbols is required to provide a detailed description of the media used in input/output activities. The system flowchart is a valuable method of communicating information flows since it displays the interrelationships of all parts of the system.

The symbols used to specify the forms of input/output on a system flowchart are miniature outlines of the actual media (Figure 4–2). The symbol for punched-card input/output looks like a small replica of a punched card. A tape is represented by a symbol that looks like a tape reel. The symbol for printed-document output resembles a torn piece of paper. Storage devices are similarly represented.

In like manner, specialized process symbols are used on a system flowchart instead of the rectangular process symbol to represent specific processing operations. For example, a trapezoid is used to indicate a manual process (Figure 4–3).

The difference in emphasis in the two forms of flowcharting is owing to the different purposes they serve. A program flowchart aids the programmer in writing a source program. It specifies the details of operation so that the program can be designed to represent the general information flow. System flowcharts often represent many operations within one process block.

Figure 4–4 diagrams the updating of an inventory file. Reports from the shipping, receiving, and production departments are received and their contents transferred onto cards. These cards and the master in-

FIGURE 4-2 System Flowcharting Input/Output Symbols

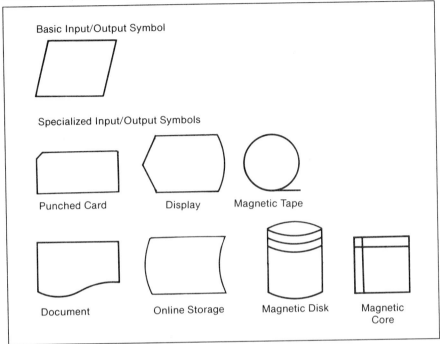

ventory file serve as input for the updating process. The output from the process includes three reports and an updated master inventory file. The symbol for the inventory file shows that it is on a direct-access storage device. Only one symbol is present since the same file serves as input and output for the updating process. The system chart indicates any data form changes, such as when data on paper is keypunched onto cards. Finally, one process block encompasses the entire updating procedure. A program flowchart must be created to detail the specific operations that would occur within the updating process.

STRUCTURED-DESIGN METHODOLOGY

As the pace of technological innovation accelerates, data-processing departments are hard-pressed to keep up. In fact, most are unable to. Software development is far behind existing technology, because it is extremely labor-intensive. Thus, data-processing departments today face a productivity problem: they must obtain greater software development for each dollar invested. The basic ways of increasing productivity are: (1) to automate the software-development process, (2) to require employees to work harder or longer or both, or (3) to change the way things

FIGURE 4–3 System Flowcharting Process Symbols

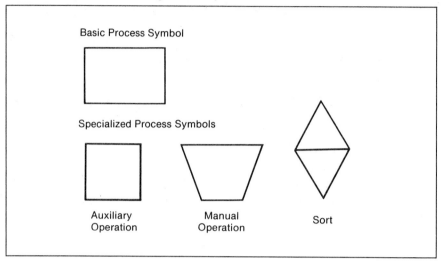

are done. Structured design attempts to achieve greater productivity by focusing on the third method.

Top-down design is a structured approach to system design. It attempts to simplify a problem by breaking it down into logical segments, or modules. The solution to a problem is first defined in terms of the functions it must perform. Each of these functions is then translated into a step (or module). The correct solution to a problem may require several of these modules, which together perform the required tasks. These modules, in turn, may be further divided.

In top-down design, the most general level of organization is the main-control logic; this overall view of the problem is the most critical to the success of the solution. Modules at this level contain only broad descriptions of steps in the solution process. Several lower-level modules contain more detail as to the specific steps to be performed. Depending on the complexity of the problem, several levels of modules may be required, with the lowest-level modules containing the greatest amount of detail.

The modules of the problem solution are related to each other in a hierarchical manner. These relationships can be depicted graphically on a **structure chart.** Figure 4–5 shows a portion of such a chart for an inventory-processing application.

When top-down design is used, certain rules must be followed. First, each module should be independent of other modules; in other words, each module should be executed only when control is passed to it from the module directly above it. Similarly, once a module has been executed, control should be passed back to the module directly above.

FIGURE 4–4 Sample System Flowchart

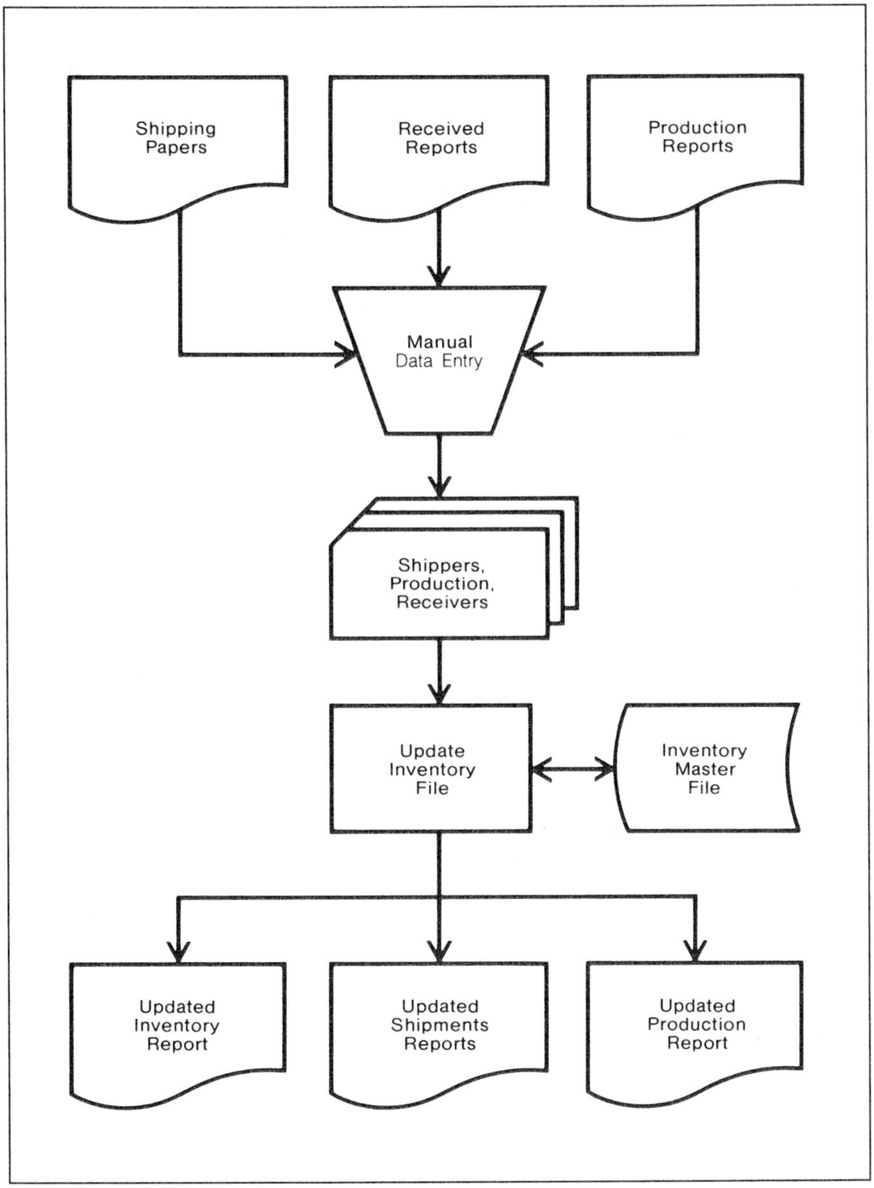

DESIGN ALTERNATIVES

The development of an MIS is an integrated approach to organizing a company's activities. The company must be structured in a way that will allow it to fully realize the benefits of integration. When considering

FIGURE 4–5 Structure Chart for Inventory-Processing
Example with Four Levels of Processing Modules

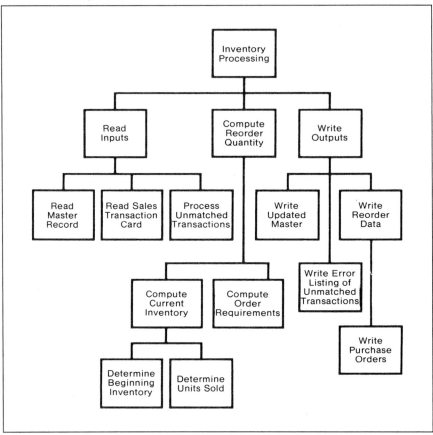

alternative organizational structures, the analyst faces virtually unlimited possibilities. This section describes four basic design structures: centralized, hierarchical, distributed, and decentralized. These structures should be viewed as checkpoints along a continuous range of design alternatives rather than as separate, mutually exclusive options.

Centralized design is the most traditional design approach. It involves the centralization of computer power. A separate electronic data-processing (EDP) department is organized to provide data-processing facilities for the organization; this department's personnel, like other staff personnel, support the operating units of the organization. All program development, as well as all equipment acquisition, are controlled by the EDP group. Standard regulations and procedures is employed. Distant units use the centralized equipment through remote access via a communication network. A common data base exists, permitting authorized users to access information (Figure 4–6a).

Several drawbacks do exist in the centralized design. Since all development and control of software and hardware are in the hands of a centralized group, the system may be slow to respond to user needs. The specialized needs of individuals in the system generally are sacrificed to meet the overall goals of the organization. Another major problem with a centralized system is that the entire system usually is paralyzed if the central computer becomes inoperative. In contrast, under other designs, equipment failure at one processing site has little or no effect on processing at other sites. In final analysis, an organization will probably want a computer system to match its management style, whether decentralized, centralized, or somewhere in between.

When **hierarchical design** is used, the organization has multiple levels with varying degrees of responsibility and decision-making authority. In hierarchical design, each management level is given the computer power necessary to support its task objectives. At the lowest level, limited support is required because the work is considered technical in nature. Middle-level support is more extensive because managerial decisions at this level require more complicated analysis (hence, more information processing). Finally, top-level executives deal with general issues that require information available only with greater processing and storage capabilities. An example of this design approach is shown in Figure 4–6b.

The **distributed-design** approach identifies the existence of independent operating units but recognizes the benefits of central coordination and control. The organization is divided into the smallest activity centers requiring computer support. These centers may be based on organizational structure, geographical location, functional operations, or a combination of factors. Hardware (and often people) are assigned to these activity centers to support their tasks. Most data is processed where it originates, and output is usually produced where it will be used. One mainframe at headquarters acts as the host computer to coordinate the processing done by the smaller, distributed systems. Total organizationwide control is evidenced by the existence of standardized classes of hardware, common data bases, and coordinated system development. The distributed computer sites may or may not share data elements, workloads, and resources, depending on whether or not they are in communication with each other. An example of the distributed-design approach is given in Figure 4–6c.

In **decentralized design,** authority and responsibility for computer support are placed in relatively autonomous organizational operating units. These units usually parallel the management decision-making structure. No central control point exists; the authority for computer operations goes directly to the managers in charge of the operating units. Since no central control is exerted, each unit is free to acquire hardware, develop software, and make personnel decisions independently. Responsiveness to user needs can be high because close working relation-

FIGURE 4–6 Sample Design Structures

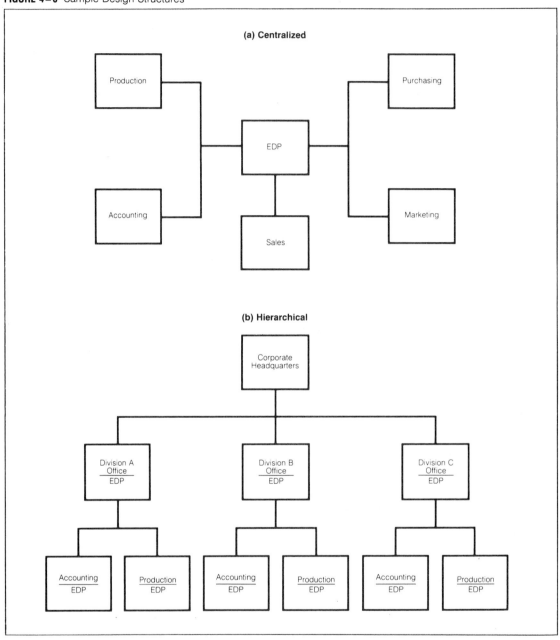

ships are reinforced by the proximity of the system to its users. Communication among units is limited or nonexistent, thereby reducing the possibility of common or shared applications. This design approach can be used only where an existing organizational structure supports de-

FIGURE 4–6 Continued

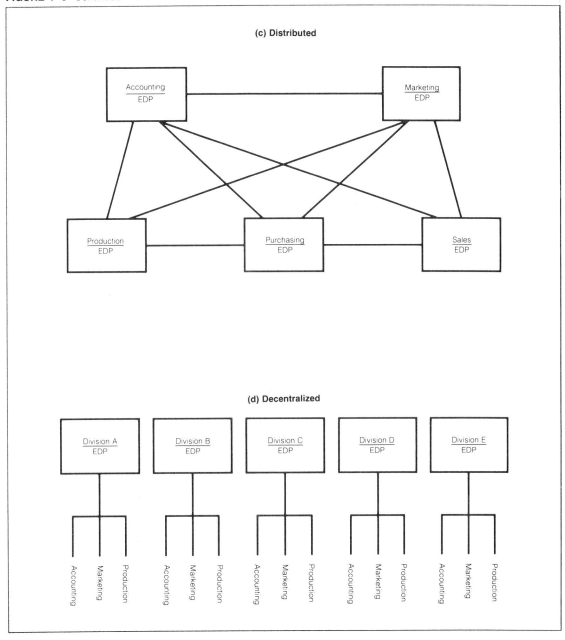

centralized management. Also, it is not highly compatible with the management-information-system concept. An example of the decentralized-design approach is shown in Figure 4–6d.

DATA-BASE MANAGEMENT

Before the integrated-system approach was introduced, departments had their own separate data files and collected their own input. In contrast, the installation of an MIS requires the use of some form of general data storage. The organization's data must be stored in such a way that the same data can be accessed by many users for varied applications. This can be accomplished by use of a **data base,** a grouping of data fields structured to fit the information needs of multiple functions of an organization. Data is independent—it is grouped and organized according to its inherent characteristics and relationships rather than specifically for one application task. Thus, numerous departments can use the data, and duplication of files is avoided.

In addition to reducing redundancy and increasing data independence, the data base increases efficiency. When a particular item is to be updated, the change needs to be made only once. There is no need for multiple updates as is required with separate files. The integration of data also permits the results of updating to be available to the entire organization at the same time. Furthermore, the data-base concept provides flexibility because the system can respond to information requests that previously may have bridged several departments' individual data files.

Data Organization

The design of data for a data base is approached from two perspectives. **Physical design** refers to how the data is kept on storage devices and how it is accessed. **Logical design** deals with how data is viewed by application programs or individual users. The logical design is performed by the system analyst and data analyst. A **data analyst** is a person assigned the task of analyzing the relationships of data in the data base. Together, they attempt to model the real-world relationships that exist among data items. Logical records should be designed independent of physical-storage considerations, so the physical design is often performed by the data-administration department. The **data-administration department** is the area responsible for maintaining the data base. Taking into account such problems as data redundancy, access time, and processing constraints, this team tries to implement the logical design within the physical records and files actually stored on the data base.

A logical unit can extend across more than one physical file. That is to say, what one user views as a logical unit of data may include data from the employee-history file and the payroll file. Conversely, one physical file may contain parts of several logical units of data. One user's logical unit may include only an employee's name and address; another may include only the employee's number and job code. In both of these cases, the data is only a part of one physical file—the employee file.

Data-Base Management System (DBMS)

To facilitate the use of a data base, an organization can use a **data-base management system (DBMS)**—a set of programs that makes data in the data base readily available to its three principal users: the programmer, the operating system, and the manager (or other information user). By installing an available DBMS, an organization greatly reduces the need to develop its own detailed data-handling capabilities.

One of the major purposes of a DBMS is to bring about the physical data independence mentioned earlier. This independence permits the physical layout of data files to be altered without necessitating changes in applications programs. Such insulation between applications and the data with which they interact is extremely desirable. The programmer does not have to pay attention to the physical nature of the file. He or she can simply refer to the specific data that the program needs. Figure 4–7 shows the application, logical, and physical views of a data-base management system.

A DBMS is not without its disadvantages, however. It can be quite costly to implement and maintain. Equipment may have to be upgraded as a DBMS requires a large memory capacity, both primary and secondary. Furthermore, access times for individual users may become slower. Yet, overall, the organization can benefit from a DBMS by having more current data, by making better use of its data, and by avoiding the need to develop complex data-handling capabilities.

COMPUTER CRIME/SECURITY

Two issues of concern to any student of the computer are computer crimes and security considerations. Computer crimes in most cases have involved using or manipulating data for personal gain and profit. Computer crimes are hard to prevent, let alone detect. Considerable effort is expended by both public and private concerns in attempts to reduce their vulnerability to crimes. Knowledge of the ways in which computer crimes have been committed will aid the system designer in developing methods to deter similar illegal access in new systems.

Computer security focuses on two main problems: how to protect the physical equipment of the computer and how to protect against unauthorized use of the computer facilities by would-be criminals. Good physical protection of the computer does not necessarily prevent criminal use of computer files. The increasing number of telecommunication facilities can provide access for the criminal desiring illegal use of the computer, even though he or she may be miles away.

Computer Crime

Computer crime is more of a problem than most people realize. Americans are losing billions of dollars to high-technology crooks whose crimes

FIGURE 4-7 Physical, Logical, and Application Views of Data

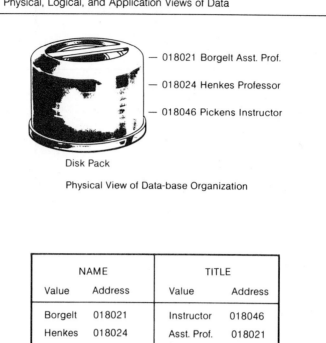

— 018021 Borgelt Asst. Prof.

— 018024 Henkes Professor

— 018046 Pickens Instructor

Disk Pack

Physical View of Data-base Organization

NAME		TITLE	
Value	Address	Value	Address
Borgelt	018021	Instructor	018046
Henkes	018024	Asst. Prof.	018021
Pickens	018046	Professor	018024

Logical View of Data-base Organization

NAME: BORGELT
TITLE: ASST. PROF.

Application of Program Files

go undetected and unpunished; estimates of losses range from at least $2 billion to more than $40 billion a year. Although no one really knows how much is being stolen, the total appears to be growing.

The earliest known instance of electronic embezzlement occurred in 1958, just a few years after IBM began marketing its first line of business computers. By the mid–1970s, scores of such crimes were being reported every year; yearly losses were estimated to be as high as $300 million.

Even worse problems appear to be ahead. Home computers and electronic funds transfer (EFT) systems pose a new threat to the billions of dollars in data banks accessible through telephone lines. Already, illegal switches of money have been made over the phone, and more cases can be expected as EFT systems become widespread.

The biggest computer crime case uncovered so far involved the Equity Funding Life Insurance Company of Los Angeles. Officers of the company used a computer to fabricate $1 billion worth of fake life-insurance accounts for 64,000 fictitious customers. They sold shares in the phony business to investors and used the computer to create the phony policies and keep track of the vast amount of data associated with them. The $2 billion fraud was discovered when a former Equity Funding employee revealed the scheme to a securities analyst, who in turn informed his clients and the authorities. When caught, the officers had at their disposal a program that could have erased all the computer evidence.

This case is only one example of the types of electronic crime being committed. Manipulating input into the computer, changing computer programs, and stealing data, computer time, and computer programs are also examples. In fact, the possibilities for computer crime seem endless. It has recently been suggested that computers are used extensively by organized crime, and that a computer-aided murder may already have taken place.

The unique threat of computer crime is that criminals often use computers to conceal not only their own identities but also the existence of the crimes. Law officers worry that solving computer crimes seems to depend on luck. Many such crimes are never discovered because company executives do not know enough about computers to detect them. Others are hushed up to avoid scaring customers and stockholders. For a company to admit that computer systems cannot be made "crime-proof" is difficult.

Only about 15 percent of computer thefts are estimated to be reported to police. Many of these do not result in convictions and jail terms because the complexities of data processing mystify most police officials, prosecutors, judges, and jurors.

To make matters worse, courts are usually lenient in sentencing computer criminals. In one exception to this almost universal rule, a bookkeeper who had stolen $1 million from his employers over six years was charged with sixty-nine counts of grand theft and forgery. He pleaded guilty and was sentenced to ten years, of which he had to serve five-and-a-half. This sentence is one of the longest ever given for a computer crime.

Computer Security

Increasing computer crime naturally spawns interest in security measures designed to deter, detect, or at best, prevent such crime. Computer security involves the technical and administrative safeguards required to protect a computer-based system (hardware, personnel, and data) against the major hazards to which most computer systems are exposed, and to control access to information.

Physical computer systems and data in storage are vulnerable to several hazards: fire, natural disasters, environmental problems, and sabotage. Fire is one of the more apparent problems because most computer installations use combustible materials–punched cards, paper, and so on. Furthermore, if a fire gets started, water cannot be used to extinguish it because water can damage magnetic-storage media and hardware. Carbon-dioxide fire-extinguisher systems are hazardous because they could endanger employees who become trapped in the computer room. Halon, a nonpoisonous chemical gas, can be used instead of carbon dioxide in fire extinguishers. Halon is more expensive, but the value of the equipment it protects can usually justify the additional cost.

Many computer centers have been damaged or destroyed by floods, cyclones, hurricanes, and earthquakes. Such natural disasters pose a serious threat to the computer hardware and wiring. Protection against natural disasters should be considered when the location for the computer center is chosen; for example, the center should not be located in an area prone to flooding.

Usually, computers are installed in buildings that were not originally planned to accommodate them. This practice can give rise to environmental problems. For example, water and steam pipes may run through a computer room; if these pipes burst, extensive damage could result. Data on magnetic media can be destroyed by magnetic fields created by electric motors in the vicinity of the computer room. Other environmental problems include power failures, brownouts (temporary surges or drops in power), and external radiation.

Sabotage represents the greatest physical risk to computer installations. Computer-center saboteurs can do great damage, with little risk of apprehension. Providing adequate security against acts of sabotage such as destroying tapes, planting bombs, or cutting communication lines is extremely difficult and expensive.

In addition to safeguarding computer systems from these physical difficulties, companies must protect stored data against illegitimate use by controlling access to it. No simple solution to these security problems exists. Organizations have instituted various security measures. Most precautions restrict access to computerized records; others provide for reconstruction of destroyed data. Some examples include: (1) storing backup copies of data outside the organization's location, (2) giving authorized users special passwords and changing them frequently, (3) allowing access to specific portions of the data base only to those whose jobs require it, (4) restricting access to the data-processing department to personnel with special badges and keys, (5) translating or encrypting data into a secret code by using complex coding devices before data is stored and decrypting it after it has been retrieved, and (6) identifying legitimate computer users by fingerprints or voice patterns.

These security measures are not complete, however. They may not prevent internal sabotage, fraud, or embezzlement. How, then, can organizations establish computer security? First, computer users must recognize their role in security. If a high-level priority is to be assigned to security in the company, employees must be made aware of such priority and of the security measures that are being taken.

Second, organizations should recognize the need to have a well-trained security force—a department of security guards who specialize in maintaining data security, conducting system audits, and asking the right kinds of questions on a daily and continuing basis.

Third, companies can exercise a great deal of care in the selection and screening of the people who will have access to computers, terminals, and computer-stored data. Companies should choose programmers as carefully as they select attorneys or accountants.

Last, organizations must discharge employees who violate company rules. Whenever incidents occur, violators must be shown that such acts will not be tolerated and that, however hard the necessary course of action, those responsible for security and protection have the intellectual and ethical integrity to follow through.

PRIVACY
Data Banks

The widespread use of computers, information systems, and telecommunication systems has created another major concern in recent years— a concern about the invasion of individual privacy. **Privacy** involves an individual's ability to determine what, how, and when information about him or her is communicated to others. Many people are concerned about the use of personal information about them by government and private business; they think that computerized recordkeeping poses a threat to personal privacy.

Before computerized recordkeeping became widespread, most business and government decisions concerning such benefits as credit, educational grants, and Medicare were based on personal knowledge of the individuals involved, on limited information obtained from a decentralized system of public records, and from friends and associates of the individuals. Thus, privacy was protected to some extent by the inefficiency of these sources and methods of collecting data. The details of people's lives were maintained in widely separated, manually maintained files and in the memories of others who knew them. To compile from these sources a detailed dossier on any individual was difficult.

With computers, data is easier to collect and store. Enabling information handlers to increase their data-collection activities tends to encourage them to collect more data. Further, computers can transmit data quickly and easily from one location to another. As mentioned earlier, manual systems provided an inherent deterrent to privacy invaders because of the difficulty of searching widely scattered records. In contrast, penetrating a single computerized data file gives access to much information, so there is greater incentive to make the attempt. Also, computers make possible the compilation of lists of people connected with various types of activities from widely scattered data that probably could not be brought together manually. Previously unknown relationships may be revealed.

"Control over personal information" has become the accepted definition of privacy. With computers, the individual often has no significant control over what personal information will be collected, whether it will be accurate and complete, or what its uses will be. In fact, the individual seldom knows that such collection and dissemination are taking place, even though such activities can effectively determine whether he or she will have access to services, medical care, and employment.

The main concerns of the privacy issue can be summarized as follows:

● Too much personal information about individuals is being collected and stored in computerized files.

● Organizations are increasingly using these computerized records in making decisions about individuals.

● Much of the personal information collected about individuals may not be relevant to the purposes for which it is to be used.

● The accuracy, completeness, and currency of the data may be unacceptably low.

● The security of stored data is a problem.

Of course, the same computers that are eroding individual privacy are also allowing institutions (private and public) to operate more efficiently. For example, it is obviously beneficial for a business to have enough information about individuals to make decisions that will control the firm's risks when issuing credit. Thus, a solution to the privacy issue must involve an appropriate balance between the legitimate needs of organizations for information about people and the rights of individuals to maintain their privacy.

Privacy Law

Since the early 1970s, an increasing number of laws and regulations to protect privacy have been enacted to control the collection, use, dissemination, and transmission of personal data. By far the most numerous have been passed by the federal government, to protect against abuse of the government's own recordkeeping agencies. The Freedom of Information Act of 1970 allows individuals to gain access to data about themselves in files collected by federal agencies. It was passed because of the government's potential to conceal its proceedings from the public.

The most sweeping federal legislation was the Privacy Act of 1974. Signed on January 1, 1975, this act was designed to protect the privacy of individuals who have information about themselves maintained by the federal government. This act stated that the individuals must be able to determine what information about themselves is being recorded by federal government agencies and how it will be used. Also, these individuals must be provided with a method of correcting or amending information that they know to be incorrect. In the same vein, information collected for one purpose should not be used for another without the consent of the individual. Finally, any organization creating, maintaining, using, or disseminating personal data must ensure the reliability of the information and must take precautions to prevent its misuse.

Although the act was a giant step in the right direction, it was criticized for its failure to reach beyond the federal government to state and private institutions. Several other laws have been passed by the federal government in an attempt to further control data-base information misuse. The Education Privacy Act is designed to protect individuals' privacy by regulating access to private and public schools' computer-stored records of grades and evaluations of behavior. The act provides that no federal funds will be made available to an educational agency that has a policy of denying parents and students the right to inspect and review the students' relevant educational records.

The Right to Financial Privacy Act of 1978 provides further protection to the individual by limiting governmental access to the customer records of financial institutions, thus protecting to some degree the confidentiality of personal financial data.

Many state laws regulating government recordkeeping practices are patterned after the Privacy Act of 1974. Most states have enacted some type of control over such practices in the public sector. Many of these laws contain provisions that require publication of notices describing the records that each governmental agency maintains; provide for the collection and storage of only data that is relevant, timely, and accurate; and prohibit unauthorized disclosures of data relating to individuals.

The only significant federal attempt to regulate the information practices of private organizations is the Fair Credit Reporting Act of 1970. This law is intended to deter privacy violations by lending institutions that use computers to store and manipulate data about people's finances. It provides to individuals the right to gain access to credit data about themselves and the opportunity to challenge and correct erroneous data.

States have also begun to regulate the information activities of nongovernmental organizations. Much of the legislation in this area operates to strengthen the protections afforded individuals by the Fair Credit Reporting Act of 1970.

Relatively few privacy-violation cases have been litigated. Since one of the problems of information privacy is that data is transferred and disclosed without the knowledge or consent of the subjects, it is not likely that people will even be aware of the use of data about themselves. Therefore, they probably will not know that they have a claim to take to court. Further, privacy litigation is something of a contradiction in terms; by taking claims to court, litigants may expose private aspects of their lives to a far greater extent than the initial intrusion did.

SOCIAL IMPACT

Computer technology has had a more significant impact on society than any other factor since the Industrial Revolution. The extent of this impact has led many to classify the present era as the **Information Revolution.** In an extremely short time period, computers have moved out of the laboratory and into an indispensable position in modern life.

This rapid progression has generated many problems as well as spectacular results. Some individuals who were born and educated before this widespread implementation of computers refuse to accept the computer's importance. Psychological barriers are raised, and no attempt is made to understand the logical base of computer operations. Technological obsolescence often requires job restructuring or retraining, which tends to increase resistance to computer applications. Computer professionals must commit themselves to continuing education if they want to remain current in such a dynamic field. These problems are people-oriented rather than dependent on scientific advancements. As such, they are more difficult to solve.

The world today would be impossible to recognize if all the advances attributed to computers were removed. For example, airlines could not continue to function without computerized airline-reservation systems; space travel would be impossible without simulation and control programs; and the U.S. economic system would grind to a halt without the tremendous speed of the computer on which the banking industry relies so heavily for processing cash flows.

But not all computer applications are beneficial or effective. The computer is only a tool used by analysts and programmers to assist in solving problems. If a solution is inappropriate or incorrect, then the computer system has the same deficiencies. Computer power is a fact of technological advancement; harnessing this power is a function of the individuals who control computer use. The principal limitation on computer application is the imagination and ingenuity of the human counterpart.

SUMMARY

● The system life cycle consists of three principal phases: system analysis, system design, and system implementation. The analysis phase starts with defining the problem and continues, after a detailed study, with formulation of information requirements. In the second phase, the analyst develops alternative designs, builds formal models of these designs, and determines the cost effectiveness of the alternatives before making recommendations. The implementation phase includes converting to the new system, testing the new system thoroughly, and training the employees who are to use it.

● A management information system (MIS) is a formal network using computer capabilities to provide management with the information necessary for decision making. The goal of an MIS is to get the correct information to the appropriate manager at the right time.

● System design may need to be based on organizational structure. Centralized design uses a central computer to perform all data-processing functions. Hierarchical design provides each level of an organization with the computing power to perform its task objectives; information becomes more summarized the higher the point in the hierarchy. Distributed design has its own computing power, yet various units must report to a central point. Decentralized design gives each part of the organization its own computing power—there is no central point of control.

● System flowcharting emphasizes the flow of data through an entire data-processing system rather than how processing is done. Because a system flowchart is designed to represent the general information flow, many operations are often represented by one process block.

● Structured design is a method of breaking down a problem into logical segments, or modules. Each module performs a logical function. These modules, in turn, may be broken down further. Modules are related to one another in a hierarchical fashion. Each module is independent of another.

● A data base is a grouping of related data fields structured to meet the information needs of a wide variety of users. Data is analyzed logically according to its inherent relationships to other data in the business setting, then designed physically for best processing. Users can relate to the logical view of data without regard to the data's physical storage.

● A data-base management system is a collection of software that provides users with access to the stored data-base data.

● The privacy issue has emerged as more and more computer files on individuals are maintained by federal, state, local, and private institutions. This issue focuses on the degree of control the individual has over personal information.

● Two issues of major concern to the student of the computer include computer crime and security.

● Most of the laws regarding the computer have been passed by the federal government and deal with the privacy issue. State laws usually reflect federal legislation and also deal with privacy. With few exceptions, there has been little attempt to regulate private business practices.

● Computer crime is more prevalent than might be suspected. Because of an unwillingness to publicize such crimes, most businesses do not prosecute such criminals. Many crimes that involve computers are concealed by the computers as well, making detection of computer crimes extremely difficult.

● Computer security focuses on two areas: physical security of the equipment and controlled access to the computer and its data. Physical security considerations involve protection from natural hazards. Efforts to prevent unauthorized access to data attempt to ensure that data is available only for its intended purpose.

● The principal limitation on computer application is the imagination and ingenuity of the human counterpart.

REVIEW QUESTIONS

1. The cornerstone of a management information system (MIS) is a(n)
   a. operating system.
   b. data base.
   c. predictive report.
   d. CPU.

2. The cost of obtaining data should never exceed the
   a. profit of the firm.
   b. information value.
   c. system analysis.
   d. operating system.

3. A data-base management system is a part of the computer
    a. software.
    b. hardware.
    c. system analysis.
    d. operating system.

4. The present era has been called the
    a. Age of Enlightenment.
    b. Industrial Revolution.
    c. Information Revolution.
    d. Renaissance.

5. Reports that monitor performance and indicate deviations from expected results are
    a. demand reports.
    b. predictive reports.
    c. scheduled listings.
    d. exception reports.

6. Which of the following is not true of an MIS?
    a. It can assist in developing more effective management.
    b. It virtually guarantees decision-making success.
    c. It reduces uncertainty.
    d. It needs user support.

7. A flowchart that designates input/output media is called a
    a. program flowchart.
    b. system flowchart.
    c. data-description flowchart.
    d. symbols flowchart.

8. An MIS is most apt to be successful when
    a. management is involved in its selection and installation.
    b. the installation incorporates all possible new technologies.
    c. one company automatically adopts an MIS similar to one used by another company in the same industry.
    d. All of the above are true of an MIS.

9. The type of MIS report that constitutes the majority of reports received is
    a. predictive.
    b. scheduled.
    c. exception.
    d. demand.

10. An integration of all data needed by an organization
    a. is done through the development of a data base.
    b. is the work of the keypunch operator.
    c. makes use of desk-checking area codes.
    d. is done after an MIS has been in operation for several months.

11. The beginning of the system life cycle starts with
    a. the correction of a malfunctioning phase in the system procedure.
    b. the advent of new technology.
    c. system design.
    d. system analysis.

12. Once a system is implemented,
    a. it remains viable until the user organization ceases to exist.
    b. it must be reviewed continually because conditions encompassing the system are always changing.
    c. a detailed program flowchart is drawn up for system documentation and for future reference in management decision making.
    d. both (a) and (c) are true of a system.

13. The Privacy Act of 1974 applies to
    a. all organizations.
    b. all public organizations.
    c. all government agencies.
    d. federal agencies.

14. Procedures to make computer systems more secure include the use of
    a. special access codes.
    b. backup data files.
    c. encryption.
    d. all of the above.

15. Which of the following is not an advantage of a data-base management system?
    a. Data redundancy is minimized.
    b. Only a small primary memory is used.
    c. Updates to data files are easily made.
    d. Direct file inquiries are possible.

16. Which design structure uses a large central computer?
    a. Distributed
    b. Hierarchical
    c. Centralized
    d. Both (b) and (c)

17. Overall, the design structure that is least responsive to users' needs is the

    a. hierarchical.
    b. distributed.
    c. centralized.
    d. decentralized.

18. An example of an exception report is a list of

    a. all employees paid during the last payroll period.
    b. the expected payrolls during the upcoming year.
    c. employees working more than sixty hours a week.
    d. all employees working for a specific department.

19. The document symbol is

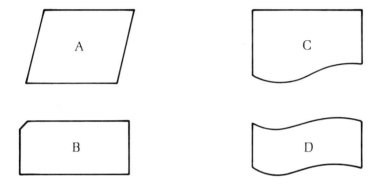

20. A fire in a computer center is best extinguished using

    a. water.
    b. a carbon-dioxide extinguisher.
    c. a Halon extinguisher.
    d. baking soda.

Glossary

Direct-access processing a method of processing in which data is submitted to the computer in the order in which it occurs; records can be located and updated without the computer having to read all preceding records on a file 22

Direct-Access Storage Devices (DASDs) auxiliary storage devices that allow data to be stored and accessed either randomly or sequentially 22

Disk drive the mechanical device used to rotate a disk pack during data transmission; common speeds range between 40 and 3,600 revolutions per second 52

Disk pack a stack of magnetic disks 52

Diskette see Floppy disk 53

Distributed design a design alternative whereby each activity center has its own computer power, although total organization-wide control exists 137

Distributed data processing system a system in which several CPUs are linked together by communication channels to form a network; this allows faster response to inquiries and provides the power to perform complex calculations 77

Documentation written descriptions of a system; include flowcharts, major processing flows, input/output forms, file designs, and a narrative 128

Dot-matrix printer also wire-matrix printer; a type of impact printer that creates characters through the use of dot-matrix patterns. 61

Downtime the time the system is not working because of equipment problems 27

Drum printer an output device consisting of a metal cylinder that contains rows of characters engraved across its surface; one line of print is produced with each rotation of the drum 62

Dumb terminal a terminal that cannot be programmed 60

EDSAC Electronic Delay Storage Automatic Computer; the first "stored-program computer." 10

EDVAC Electronic Discrete Variable Automatic Computer; performed arithmetic and logic operations without human intervention 10

Electronic data processing (EDP) data processing that is performed largely by electronic equipment such as a computer rather than by manual or mechanical methods 5

Electrostatic printer a nonimpact printer that forms an image of a character on special paper using a dot matrix of charged wires or pins; when the paper is moved through a solution containing ink particles of an opposite charge from the pattern, the particles adhere to each charged pattern on the paper 63

Magnetic tape a storage medium consisting of a narrow strip upon which magnetized spots of iron oxide are used to represent data; a sequential storage medium 13

Magnetic-disk storage a storage medium consisting of a metal platter coated on both sides with a magnetic recording material upon which data is stored in the form of magnetized spots; suitable for direct-access processing 22

Magnetic-ink character reader a device that reads characters composed of magnetized particles; often used to sort checks for subsequent processing 56

Magnetic-Ink Character Recognition (MICR) the process that allows magnetized characters to be read by a magnetic-ink character reader 56

Mainframe another name for the central processing unit (CPU) 3

Management information system (MIS) a formal network that extends computer use beyond routine reporting and into the area of management decision making; its goal is to get the correct information to the appropriate manager at the right time 130

Mark I the first automatic calculator 8

Master file a file that contains relatively permanent data; updated by records in a transaction file 20

Megabyte one million bytes—a unit of computer storage 38

Message-switching a communications processor with the principal task of receiving messages and routing them to appropriate destinations 70

Microcomputer a computer on a chip (small circuit board) 17

Microprocessor circuitry on a miniature-sized chip equivalent to the CPU of a full-sized computer 15

Microprogramming the process of building a sequence of instructions into read-only memory to carry out functions that would otherwise be directed by stored program instructions at a much slower speed 45

Microsecond 1/1,000,000 second; a term used in specifying the speed of electronic devices 38

Millisecond 1/1,000 second; a term used in specifying the speed of electronic devices 38

Minicomputer a computer with the components of a full-sized system but having a smaller memory 13, 72

Modem also called data set; a device that modulates and demodulates signals transmitted over communication facilities 26

Modulation a technique used in modems to make business-machine signals compatible with communication facilities 26

Monitor another name for the supervisor program 88

†